TRUE SON
OF HEAVEN

How Jesus Fulfills the
Chinese Culture

David B. Marshall

KUAI MU
PRESS

ACKNOWLEDGEMENTS

Only my name appears on the cover of this book, and any errors are my responsibility alone. I would like to thank the many people who have contributed to the success of this book, however. In particular, I would like to thank my wife Mayumi for her patience, my parents John and Pat Marshall for taking in three refugees, Rand and Laurel Marshall for their help in many ways, Dr. James Taylor and Don Richardson for their valuable suggestions, Bob Colvin, Dr. Ohki, Samuel Wei, Masato and Chiziko Fukushima, and Elaine Colvin, probably the most generous person I know.

CONTENTS

GLOSSARY

A Note About The Chinese Language:

In spoken Mandarin Chinese each sound can be pronounced five different ways. In English we need to represent many sounds then with the same letters. For this reason, Chinese has many words which when written in English appear to be the same, but are not. The following glossary uses the pinyin system of mainland China. "I" is pronounced ee, "ao" is "ow," "a" is like a in "bald," "u" is "oo," and "x" is close to "s."

Avalokitsvara: Indian term for a Buddhist god.

Bodhisattva: Buddhist term for a Savior.

Chang Shou: "Long Life."

Dan Wei: work unit, usually in Mainland China.

Di: Ancient name for God, still in use as "Shang Di," God, and the emperor's name.

Fu: Happiness, prosperity.

Fuku: Japanese pronunciation for Fu.

Gu Gong: "Ancient palace," the home of emperors during the last two dynasties, from about 1420 to 1910.

Hao: "Good."

Huang Tian Shang Di: "Awesome Heaven God Above," one of several names for God in Chinese.

Kong: Empty.

Kong Zi, Kong Fu Zi: Confucius.

Kou: Mouth.

Lao Wai: "Old outside," foreigner, somewhat familiar.

Li: About half of one kilometer.

Mama huhu: So-so, not bad.

Mantou: A steamed bun of bread.

Maya: Sanskrit for "empty."

Nei: Inside.

Ren: Person.

Renao: "Hot and noisy," boisterous, lively.

Shang Di: One of four modern names often used for God. Sometimes used of exalted Taoist deities, with an additional name added.

Shen: Another name for God, or gods.

Shuyu: Consort.

Tai Chi: A slow-motion exercise, originally with occultic connotations.

Tao (Dao): The Way, road.

Tian: Heaven, God, day.

Wai: Outside.

Wai Guo Ren: "Out Country Person." Foreigner.

Wen: Culture.

Wo: I.

Xiao, Zhong Xiao: Loyalty, faithfulness, "filial piety."

Yi: One.

Yang Jiao: "Foreign teaching." Contemptuous.

Zi: Child.

Is Jesus foreign religion?

Chapter One

Is Jesus "Foreign Religion"?

Does Christianity belong in the Far East? I believe not only can the Gospel be reconciled to China, but that God's fingerprints are all over Chinese culture. He has, in fact, prepared it for the news of Jesus Christ.

The idea that China has been set up for Christianity may sound a bit outrageous at first. The words of British author Rudyard Kipling, "East is East, and West is West, and never the twain shall meet" sound more reasonable to many in both east and west.

The Boxer Rebellion of a century ago seemed to sum up what a lot of Chinese once felt about the subject. China had been torn apart by imperialist European powers, forced to trade in opium, and to add insult to injury, asked to politely host Westerners who came to tell her about a God of love.

In 1900, public opinion was whipped to a frenzy by a radical secret society, the "Boxers." An order to kill missionaries and their converts winged across China from the Empress Dowager. The common people responded gladly. In Shansi Province, one band of retreating Christians were attacked in every village, beaten, robbed of all their money, stripped naked, and threatened with death. In one town, an old man hurled this taunt at them:

> "Jesus, Jesus. What do we want with your Jesus? We mean to drive you 'foreign devils' out of China and Jesus too. Away with Him, and away with you!"[1]

1

From his point of view, it was reasonable to think Jesus would leave with these tall, pale foreigners. He'd come with them, hadn't he?

And what had they brought? Foreign soldiers and opium. Missionaries who offended the gods with their impious talk—which was why drought had come that year—and, it was said, used the eyes of children to make medicine.

Today, most Chinese are more polite. Yet in their hearts, many still feel, as one young Taiwanese man told me, the Christian God "Wears a foreign face." A poll I conducted in Taiwan showed about eighty percent of the people there agree Christianity is *yang jiao*, foreign religion.

Sometimes even Chinese Christians seem to feel Jesus "wears a foreign face."

Santa Claus Is Coming To Preach

Chiang Kai Shek Memorial Park is an oasis of Chinese beauty in the otherwise grey and dismal modern city of Taipei, Taiwan. Brightly-colored carp swim under willow trees. Local people paint, practice *tai chi*, or stroll in the park with friends. Near Sun Yat Sen gate, the towering crimson pillars and gold tiles of the National Theater and National Music Hall remind Chinese of the wealth of their artistic heritage.

One Christmas Day, I watched a group of about twenty Chinese Christians stand on the steps under those pillars dressed in Santa Claus outfits. Old English and German melodies filtered out from under their white cotton beards. Then their leader took a microphone and began urging spectators to put their faith in a Jew named *Yesu*.

These young men and women were sincere in their desire to "Bring China to Christ." Many had been treated like traitors to their traditions, some even cast out of their homes, for their faith. But it seemed they, too, found it difficult to separate the Christian faith from western culture.

If anyone watching followed Santa into a local church, his initial impression that Christianity was un-Chinese would likely grow. Many churches look like they belong in a medieval European city or the Vermont countryside. Pastors sprinkle English, German or Latin into sermons.

Many in Taiwan admire Christianity. "Christians are quick to care for others," one admitted. "Their lifestyles are relatively controlled," another told me. "'Jesus teaching' is good, like all religions," many agreed.

"But we have some of the worlds' deepest philosophy, and thousands of gods and goddesses. Do we really need this foreigner, sage though he may have been?"

Statue in Xiamen Harbor (Amoy) of Warlord Cheng Gong, who drove the Dutch off of Taiwan. Nationalist-occupied islands lie about five miles away. The rulers of Taiwan have often been called by the communists "puppets" of the Americans and threatened with forced expulsion.

Bringing Divine Truths From Other Lands

Many Westerners also feel troubled or embarrassed at Christian missions. "Does everyone need to believe the same?" They ask. "Why require people to give up their own prophets and wise men to accept a western Savior?"

Some western intellectuals feel the absurdity of preaching European doctrines to China with special intensity. After all, this is the land of Confucius and Lao Zi, the origin of paper, modern kilns, and gun powder, whose grand public projects and remarkable art work defined civilization while great European cities were still rude market towns. What does she need our religion for?

After discovering the beauty of traditional Chinese music, American writer Bill Holms felt a need for Western humility:

"China is not just another culture; it is another planet, intellectually. . . It is one thing to read abstractly that you are not the center of the universe, and that truth, divine or otherwise . . . was not dropped exclusively in your lap, for your personal

3

amusement and salvation. The lesson to be learned from these shocks is to cultivate modesty and curiosity and to eschew evangelism and certainty." [2]

China certainly has much to teach the world.

But can any nation really be "another planet?" China has tried, from time to time. Yet those periods in her history when she shut the door tightest against the outside world are not the eras she is most proud of. The most controversial and stirring work in China in recent years was a television series called *Cruel River*. Its thesis was that like the Yellow River on which Chinese civilization was built, China needs to flow "to the deep blue sea," [3] to mix with other nations. Deng Xiao Ping's economic policy has brought China to life by allowing outside money and work ethic to stir up China's economic waters.

No one can ask China to stop being Chinese. But are there no other "divine truths" besides economic laws to which all cultures must adjust? Helms himself seemed to think his students ought to hear his ideas on democracy.

Before a farmer sows seed, he plows the soil. Before a builder lays a foundation, he works the ground beneath it. If God cared about the human race enough to reveal facts of vital importance to our spiritual well-being, would He not likewise prepare the people of the world for them beforehand? Truth of truly divine origin would be universal.

Over the last forty years, Chinese communists have shown a zeal like that of the Boxers for doing away with "Western" religion. It is increasingly evident they did not succeed. In the last few years, tens of millions of people in mainland China have become Christians.

It is not a foreign religion which so many Chinese are now embracing. God has furrowed deep in the souls of the Chinese and planted seeds of His grace. Christianity is the fulfillment of what China has known to be true for thousands of years.

"I Have Been Here All Along"

I first caught a hint of this fact on a hot summer day in 1984, during my first visit to the Temple of Heaven in Beijing.

It was a beautiful building. Three roofs rose one above the other like a wedding cake, with frosting so blue it seemed to have drained the pigment from the sky. Four red and gold pillars, twelve red pillars in a circle around them, and twelve more in a wider circle inside the wall, held these layers in place. Under the eaves, where swallows flew in and out, the ceiling was carved in intricate, colorful patterns.

The people who built the Temple of Heaven—the first rulers of the Ming Dynasty—wanted above all for Chinese religion to wear a Chinese face. The Ming emperors threw off the yoke of the Mongols, chased foreigners out of the capital, and put up this hall as a revival of pure Chinese beliefs.

The building should have been as alien to me as anything on earth. Yet in odd ways, it seemed familiar. The inside pillars reminded me of four gold-leafed red-letter edition Gospels. The red outer pillars suggested the twelve patriarchs and twelve apostles of the Bible—symbolized in Christian writings by pillars sprinkled with blood.

Here, I learned, like the high priest in Jerusalem, one man came once a year to ask pardon for a nation. Whom did he appeal to? *"Tian:"* a Supreme God identified with Heaven who could not be represented by idols. As in Jerusalem, here, too, the sacrifice of animals would bring Heaven's mercy. The emperor even brought many of the same creatures to the altar.

It was familiar. But not like the dreams I dreamt as a child, in a basement bedroom where I knew every musty smell and could find my way in the dark. It was like when I woke in the morning and saw sunlight on poplar trees outside. A light common to man, ancient but fresh as the dawn, seemed to bathe me. I felt its rays on my heart, not a private dream, but shining on all who wake.

As I descended the steps of the temple, a Voice seemed to speak to me: "I didn't just come with the missionaries. I have been here all along. I made China."

In the eleven years since, I've gotten to know China better. I studied Mandarin, China's "common tongue," and other dialects. I wandered China on bicycle, skiff, airplane, hydrofoil, ferry, tractor, and tired old buses and trains. I walked for three weeks across Taiwan. I ate, prayed, studied, hitchhiked, and got sea sick with Chinese friends. I visited cities of millions and counties that hadn't seen another American for decades. I read China's great thinkers. I visited Buddhist and Taoist temples and talked till my throat was soar. And I listened, too.

The more I listened, the clearer I heard God's voice. He seemed to say: "I haven't forgotten China. I made her for My Son."

The Gospel is not the first "foreign" ideology to move the Chinese.

Over the centuries, China has been touched for better as well as for worse by outsiders who came proclaiming "eternal truths." Three teachers from outside have done more than any others to shape China: Buddha, Karl Marx, and Jesus Christ.

As we will see in the following chapters, the first two moved China from the outside, like a cue ball striking billiards. Buddhism was too foreign for China to accept as was—so Chinese changed it. Marxism was too foreign to accept China as was—so it changed China. Both moved China, to a certain extent. Both even moved her in positive directions. But both moved her from the outside.

At first glance, Christianity, with its organs and three-piece suits and systematic theology and gothic architecture, doesn't just seem foreign in China. It seems out-of-place, like Santa singing "Hark, the Herald Angels Sing" by a pagoda.

But Jesus moves China from the inside, like a hand in a glove, or a key in a lock. He provides workable answers to a series of riddles that have been troubling China for millennia. His life brings out deep meaning which symbols of Chinese civilization have hinted at all along. The links between the Gospels and China are varied, complex, and unmistakably planned. In the following chapters, as we look one by one at the key concepts in Chinese thinking, we will see that just as the Temple standing above the Beijing horizon reminds those who look closely of the Christian God, so the most important symbols and ideas of the Chinese culture point to Jesus.

Things You Can't Miss In China

What are the outstanding features of Chinese culture? What artifacts, customs and patterns of action do visitors notice first? Are these the same as what Chinese themselves take most pride in?

Rock or fire might catch a tourist's eye first.

In Beijing and the older capital of Xian, everything old seems made of stone: the Great Wall, the Forbidden City, the cobblestones of Tiananmen Square. The enormous grave of Qin Shi Huang, who united China two thousand years ago, is built into the earth like the work of a lost race of dwarves. At a Chinese night market, customers shout and laugh around tables piled high with foods cooked over flaming woks. Fireworks explode as a new store is opened and friends unwind for a holiday. What we call china, too, emerges from furnaces invented by the Middle Kingdom.

On second glance, softer images might catch his attention. In the haze of China's temples, among hundreds of dark idols, a radiant lady in white, or a gold figure with hundreds of arms, often stand out from the crowd. These are common forms of *Guan Yin Pu Sa*, China's most popular goddess.

Other symbols of Chinese culture lie further off the beaten track. Let a visitor brave the cold mists, freeloading monkeys, and gauntlets of entrepreneurs up the trails of China's awesome holy mountains. Let him visit the hometown of Confucius in Shandong Province. Let him trace China's ancient trade link to the outside world, the Silk Road in the dry Northwest. I've traveled in China for twelve years, and still a new surprise seems to wait around every bend of a river or curve of a road.

Along the way I've rubbed shoulders with people who told me more about China: teachers who spent decades in prison and wait out their days in the park. Chain-smoking young businessmen. Retired soldiers who snuck by sleeping American G.I.s in the Korean War or took part in China's assault on Vietnam. Expansive communist party officials on vacation. Farmers who offered a stalk of sugar cane or a ride on a tractor to the next village.

The Temple of Heaven, the Great Wall, the Forbidden City, holy mountains, Confucius, Guan Yin, the tastes, the sounds, the colors of China—each is obvious because it's famous, and it's famous because these people care about it. Talk to the folk strolling the streets; crowding onto buses; clanging bicycles loaded with watermelons, windows or even willow trees through the streets; calling you to buy paintings, handbags or fruit; or making conversation on the train. They inherit this culture. They will pass it along, altered by their passions and character, to the next generation. China remains a puzzle with many pieces, for each person you meet in China is also a piece of that puzzle.

The Face That Pulls Chinese Culture Together

Looking at these and other facets of Chinese culture is like flying over central China in late spring. The sun reflects off rice fields below in a hundred disjointed fragments, broken by levies and by growing rice. Yet together these bits and pieces of flooded earth reflect back hints of a single familiar shape. When we look at Chinese culture, it also may seem to be formed of unrelated elements. But a single face brings those bits and pieces together.

For three thousand years, China has been trying to meet the man whose face this is. Chinese kings climbed to look for him on mountain tops. Later "Sons of Heaven" acted out the climatic scenes of his life when they walked from the Forbidden City to the Temple of Heaven. China's greatest thinker caught sight of him from a distance, as in a vision. His disciples and rivals heard echoes of his voice coming, they thought, from opposite directions. Peasants looked for him in temples around China.

Of course the Boxers and Communists could not cast Jesus out of China. Chinese culture itself is a picture of his face, shattered in pieces like a puzzle.

The Chinese Communists fragmented their own culture, in an effort to remake it in their image. But now, as Chinese pick up broken pieces of tradition, and decide what to save and what to leave, many are finding Jesus. His face draws the deepest truths in Chinese civilization together in a surprising mosaic that makes sense of each part.

Rudyard Kipling's poem is usually misquoted, by the way. He does say East and West "never shall meet." But in the next line he gives this breathtaking prophecy: "Till earth and sky stand presently / At God's great judgement seat." [5]

This is the point at which we will start.

China always believed in a God who judges mankind. China believed God's love or anger depended on how we followed the *Tao*, the "Way" of right living. A man who lived two thousand six hundred years ago in Shandong Province did more than anyone in China to point people to this Way. His name was Confucius. He lived near a place where Chinese believed heaven and earth stood together—a rocky outcrop called Mount Tai.

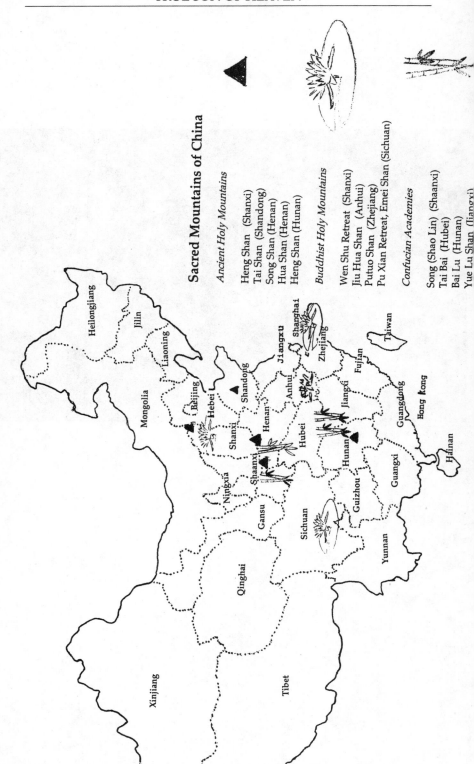

Sacred Mountains of China

Ancient Holy Mountains

Heng Shan (Shanxi)
Tai Shan (Shandong)
Song Shan (Henan)
Hua Shan (Henan)
Heng Shan (Hunan)

Buddhist Holy Mountains

Wen Shu Retreat (Shanxi)
Jiu Hua Shan (Anhui)
Putuo Shan (Zhejiang)
Pu Xian Retreat, Emei Shan (Sichuan)

Confucian Academies

Song (Shao Lin) (Shaanxi)
Tai Bai (Hubei)
Bai Lu (Hunan)
Yue Lu Shan (Jiangxi)

Part II

Tao: "The Way Of Heaven"

Gathering to climb Yellow Mountain.

Chapter Two

The Sun Rise From Mount Tai

One of the best ways to get to know China and her people is to climb one of her holy mountains. China's peaks, far from being wilderness experiences or peaceful retreats where you can "get away from it all," are people places. Along the trails, talkative vendors set up displays of beer, soft drinks, t-shirts, wall-hangings, jewelry, tapestries of tigers, pictures of Buddha, medicinal roots, and mushrooms that keep hearts ticking to the top. Porters, with muscles like molten bronze, and necks bent forward like wind-sculpted mountain firs, sling enormous stones on bamboo poles between their shoulders, or cart tired mountaineers on chairs. Others haul bundles of food or even doors for new mountain hostels step by painful step up the sheer paths.

Half the dialects of China echo in the mountain air. At the numerous rest stops, intellectuals from think tanks in Beijing, students from Shanghai and Canton, wealthy farmers, and businessmen smoke, drink tea, and crack sunflower seeds. A hiker with white skin and a tall nose, like all unusual sights, is fodder for tea-table commentary.

"A foreigner! You don't see one of those too often."

"Try your English out on him!"

"What country do you suppose 'Old Outside' is from?"
"England, I bet."

13

"Do you think he'll make it to the top?"
"I don't know. Looks pretty tired."

"Why doesn't he take the tram?"

"Go, Old White!"

Unlike American ranges, which run north to south, mountains in China seem to boil up all over like a pot of water. Several peaks in different corners of the country have become repositories of Chinese culture, shaping Chinese imagination with their special beauty. Towering Mount Emei in the Southwest is covered with Buddhist monasteries. Puto on the coast south of Shanghai is the legendary birthplace of China's beloved goddess, Guan Yin. Yellow Mountain in Anhui Province, with soaring cliffs and sheer, never-ending stairs of stone, pine and mist-soaked rhododendrons, continues to inspire China's landscape painters.

The scenery on these peaks still fires the imagination of climbers as it lures them towards the clouds. Cliffs shaped like monkeys or Buddhas or beautiful women loom out of the fog, each with its own story. The calligraphy of ancient graffiti artists calls from rock faces, beckoning visitors to "The Cave of Heaven Blessing the Earth" or "The Fount of Living Water." Another promises "Exquisite and awesome beauty." Some cliffs offer caution: "Only the brave climb to the divine place." "Slowly enter the wonderful site." Others give encouragement. "Those who ask will receive." "You need to experience it for yourself."

Experience what? Receive what? What do people who crowd to these out-of-the-way crags come to see? What "exquisite and awesome" sight awaits at the top of China's holy peaks?

The sunrise, to begin with.

Meeting The Day From The Summit

Yellow Mountain was the first sacred peak I climbed in China. My second morning, the hostel I was staying in—near the famous "Welcoming Pine"—emptied early. I slept. It'd been a long climb. Later in the day, fellow-hikers dropped enticing and mysterious hints of what I'd missed: "cloud seas," "Yellow River golden thread," a "Morning jade glow." The next morning, at Beijing Park, I dashed cold water on my face and clambered outside.

I wasn't alone in the darkness. Tuffs of rock and even pine trees were covered with other early birds. Rocky outcrops on the edge of the clearing where the old hostel lay were standing-room only.

The horizon lightened. It was a bit overcast, so I couldn't see the Yellow River or the surface fog that create or facilitate the optic

Mountains of Eastern Taiwan: mystery and beauty.

phenomena so popular on Chinese mountains. The sun rose, blurred but glorious above the hazy horizon. The clear mountain air was filled with clapping and cheering.

My hands and face were chilled, but my heart warmed. What human production can match the simple drama and beauty of a sunrise from the top of a mountain?

A few months later, I lived in a musty dormitory in the basement of "Taipei Mountain Church." I slept next to Chinese-speaking mountain people, young Amei, Taya and Paiwan tribal men, in a row on a plywood shelf.

Every morning as I lay in bed, at about five-thirty I heard singing, clapping, loud praying and the soft thump of an electric guitar from the next room. Some mornings my roomates danced to greet the new day.

Years later, on a morning climb up the greatest of China's sacred peaks, one of the tribal songs they sang ran through my mind and pulsed out on my lips as a silent hum:

"I will lift my head up to Heaven, I will lift up my head to Heaven. My help comes from there. From the One who created Heaven and Earth. . . *Ah-yau-eyo-ei* from Jehovah it comes."

The next line was a savage but cheerful yell. At the moment, I was too winded to open my mouth. But the awesome rocky cliffs rising above both sides of the trail seemed to echo the shout in my heart.

I was climbing Mount Tai.

A Blank Stone on Mount Tai

Tai Shan divides Shandong peninsula just west of Korea from the interior part of Shandong province. It isn't particularly tall; exactly five thousand feet at the summit. The lower half is covered with cedar. The upper half towers dramatically in the late afternoon sun, rocky and inaccessible-looking.

The name "Mt. Tai" has entered the Chinese language as "a symbol of great weight or importance." "Tai Shan and the Big Dipper" refers to a "VIP." It's said that "A time comes for every man to die, but his death may be as weighty as Mt. Tai, or as light as a feather." A stone inscription about halfway up declares "Mt. Tai—the first mountain under Heaven."

What is so special about this place?

Men once climbed the holiest of China's mountains in search of—holiness.

On any mountain, get up early and you may see the sun. But here, like the young mountain tribesmen in that church, ancient Chinese sages arose to greet the One who made it.

Mount Tai is like a Chinese Mount Sinai. Here, too, Heaven's precepts were carved in stone. Here China's prophets and rulers came to make their deal with God.

This is the pulpit China's three greatest leaders: Confucius, Emperor Qin, and Mao Tse Tung—mounted to deliver their shortest and plainest sermons. It was the chapel where they lifted their eyes to the Creator—or looked away.

****

I came in late summer, after the hottest part of the year. I took a pre-dawn bus to Middle Heaven Gate and hiked to the summit, the rising sun over my shoulder. Gentle slopes near the top were covered with pink, white and bright blue wild flowers, with ash trees and rhodedendrums scattered on the far slope. Fog moved in and out among the big rocks at the top.

All along the trail stood temples to various gods and goddesses of Chinese legend. Along the final ridge before the summit, the trail bisected a large complex dedicated to the Azure Princess, a popular northern Chinese goddess. At the summit lay a temple for the Jade Emperor, the Taoist Zeus.

16

Climbing Mount Tai with goods.

Outside this temple, though, stood a single, plain stone obelisk about fifteen feet high. There were no words or images on it.

A tour guide told me this was the oldest man-made object on the mountain, older than any temple or writings in the rocks. Probably it was the emperor Han Wu Di who ordered it erected. Han Wu Di was China's Constantine: the man who, after a period of intense persecution, made a popular new teaching that put a new spin on old ideals safe for the empire. A little too safe, some say: in Han's hands, Confucianism developed a kind of spiritual beer-belly, like Christianity under Constantine.

But Han Wu Di himself was not a lazy man. However vague or pragmatic his belief in God might have been, he climbed Mount Tai seven times to pay honor to Him. The emperor asked his scholars to think of a fitting inscription for such a holy spot. Nothing they came up with seemed quite right. So he left the monument blank. Finding it difficult to express what he had to say in words, he replaced them with an act, as later Zen Masters would so often do. Perhaps he was thinking of the Taoist "uncarved block," the ultimate essence from which all things derive.

Mt. Tai: Where Heaven meets Earth.

One way up the mountain.

"The first mountain
under Heaven."

The God China Knew

The Apostle Paul found an altar with the inscription "To an unknown god" on a hill above Athens. He told the people who gathered to hear him there, "What you worship in ignorance, I am now going to tell you about."[1]

Centuries before the time of Paul and of Han Wu Di, China also climbed a hill to worship the Almighty. But you could hardly say God was "unknown" to the Chinese.

Chen Jingpan, Academic Commitee Consultant of the China Confucian Foundation, wrote,

> "From the very ancient days of Chinese history, down through the time of Confucius to the present, we have records about the Chinese belief in one supreme God, the ruler over heaven and earth."[2]

The words Chinese used for God were *Tian* and *Shang Di*.

Tian means "heaven" or "sky." It also means the Power behind the heavens—God, in other words. *Shang* means "upper" or "go up." A Chinese-English dictionary defines *Di* as "The Supreme Being."[3]

Throughout history, China has felt the Presence of One whose nature images carved in wood or even words carved in stone seemed inadequate to express. He wasn't like "gods" and "goddesses" of popular legend. I doubt China took most of its myths much more seriously than we take soap operas. As Frena Broomfeld said, the Chinese gods "Are there to be fooled, and the Chinese are there to fool them."[4]

But Chinese literature warned against trifling with Heaven:

> "In public matters men cannot be deceived, in matters of the heart *Tian* cannot be deceived."[5]

> "Telling secrets in a private room is heard by *Tian* like thunder."[6]

Maybe this is why Han Wu Di was left without words, or why no one tried to carve idols of *Tian*, as with other "gods."[7]

Some claim *Tian* was an "impersonal force" to the Chinese, not God as Christians think of Him. One Western writer claimed the term meant only "An abstract concept of universal harmony."[8] But a Chinese philosophical reference work says to the contrary *Tian* first of all "Refers to a personal, volitional God."[9]

19

The personal character of God is clear in ancient Chinese writings, like these sayings from the era of the Jewish prophets:

"Great Heaven is very intelligent." [10]

"How great is the love of Heaven towards the people!" [11]

Tian took an active interest in mankind:

"Let me not say that He is high aloft above me, He ascends and descends about our doings; He daily inspects us "[12]

In practically every way, *Tian* resembled the God of the Bible. He cared for the weak and the helpless. He punished evil and rewarded good. He couldn't be represented by an idol.

Did the Chinese think of *Tian/ Shang Di* as Creator? Peoples who live in the south of China, such as the Hani (Akha), Lahu, and Lisu passed down stories of how God created all things. Tribal peoples in Taiwan also thought of God as Creator and Judge of mankind. The Buddhist Dai of Xishuangbanna near Burma preserve an epic which in Chinese is called "The Creation Poem." When I began learning their language, I discovered its original title is "In the Beginning gods created the world." (Or "God." Dai, like Chinese, mutes the distinction between singular and plural.)

Chinese literature holds hints of God's creation, too. The *Book of Poetry*, the most ancient collection of Chinese literature, exclaims, "Oh, vast and distant Heaven, who are called our parent." Also, "Heaven gave me birth."[13]

In Taiwan, I found that though only one person in the hundred I polled was a Christian, more than a third believed in a God who created the universe. Many others were unsure. God often seemed distant or a bit vague to the Chinese, but never really unknown.

The Temple of Heaven is an unmistakable reminder of that. The first emperors of the Ming dynasty, having chased Genghis Khan's great-grandchildren out of China, built this magnificent worship hall to restore *Chinese* religion. In it they placed a plaque which united both names of God in one: *Huang Tian Shang Di*, "Awesome Heavenly Supreme Being."

But the earliest and holiest spot at which man could meet God in China appears to have been Mt. Tai. Before bricks for any of the temples on the mountain were carted up, before the mortals who would be worshiped in those temples were even born, let alone attained immortality in the popular imagination, and at least a thousand years before Han Wu Di stood speechless at the summit, men came here to honor their "Parent in Heaven."

Does China Still Need Holy Mountains?

One reason hikers keep to the main path at the top of Mt. Tai is that the bushes have been used as a garbage dump. Why do some hikers care so little for this sacred peak?

Perhaps that's a feudal complaint, as the communists say. Who looks for holiness in a hill anymore? Better to look for copper or gold. Climbers "conquer" Mt. Everest and leave Coke cans behind. The materialistic bent of Marxist ideology in China and secular thinking in the West both seem to sap romance from the popular imagination.

A short while ago, a comet plunged towards Jupiter's surface. Satellites positioned to photograph the crash. What would they learn about comets and the atmosphere of gaseous planets? Scientists asked. Would a new red spot appear?

Ancient poets might have asked instead what the lords of the sky were up to, and what revolutions and disasters were likely to follow on earth.

Maybe the ancients read too much into little things. But many today fail to read anything at all into realities that tower over our souls like mountains.

The universe was determined by a burst of atoms ten billion years ago, Chinese have been taught for forty years. The movements of the stars, the development of life, the thoughts in our brains, are the fixed effects of those blind causes. What follows? Love is a hormone. Worms are the ultimate winners. One skeptic said, "Philosophy has been thought through to an end."[14]

Yet many with a scientific education in today's China look around at the world and can't help but see "more than is dreamt of" in atheist philosophy, whether of the ancient Chinese rationalist Xun Fei Zi or of Karl Marx.

I met a science teacher of retirement age in a Shanghai park. He'd been raised on nothing but materialism and evolution. But, he told me, it "only made sense" that there was a Creator.

What science causes, science often helps cure.

If mountains and comets no longer awe you, climb Mount Tai anyway. Bring a microscope. Look in a little mudpuddle in the crack of the rock near the summit. In a single drop of that brackish water, modern technology finds as much to wonder at as the ancients found in all the stars in heaven. A scientist of Thomas Edison's day could have taken his first light bulb apart and figured it out in days. Yet the world's top scientists have spent millions of hours trying to work out the structure of microscopic creatures like the smallest in that puddle. They are stymied not only by a bacteria's size, but by the exquisite complexity and precision of the mechanisms that allow it to squirm, search for food and digest it, expell waste, protect its integrity, and reproduce.

Now examine the feather of a crow that lands to watch—a miracle of aerodynamic genius aircraft engineers can only envy. Look in the eye of a hawk circling below. Watch a grain of corn in the plains beneath hatch out of the ground and grow into a seedling. Take a close look at a banana leaf, or a mosquito's drill, or a fire-fly's lamp.

Or wait with the crowd at the top of the mountain for the sun to come up. Every infant knows the first wonder is light itself.

American Surgeon General C. Everett Koop found *Shang Di* with a scalpel:

> "I never operate without having a subconscious feeling that there's no way this extraordinarily complicated mechanism known as the human body just happened to come up from slime and ooze someplace. When I make an incision with my scalpel, I see organs of such intricacy that there simply hasn't been enough time for natural evolutionary processes to have developed them."[15]

For those whose eyes are open, the fingerprints of God on life are everywhere in creation.

Some find God in the complexity of living systems, others in their beauty. For others, existence itself argues a First Cause. Thinkers from Mo Zi in ancient China to Oxford philosopher C. S. Lewis, have detected God's voice in the conscience of man. Others, including farmers and officer workers I met in central China and Taiwan, find Him through miracles.

Awe is still the natural response with which a man with an open mind faces the universe. But to see the Light, one must walk the *Tao*, the path or road, all the way to the summit.

Is There Only One Way To The Top?

Above the tree line, the wind blows free. The world and its cares are at your feet, small and distant. A pure blue quilt hangs over your head. Weightless, it seems to press on you with its mystery; distant, you want to reach out and touch its eternal light. It radiates hope into your heart, but a kind of shyness too.

A Chinese proverb expresses the paradox of such a moment. A perfect man "Hears the roll of thunder, but is not afraid," but, "sees the blue sky above him, and fears."[16]

The Hebrew "Book of Poetry," the *Psalms*, also speaks of a fear that comes when danger passes. "If you, O Lord, kept a record of sins, who could stand? But there is forgiveness with you. Therefore may you be feared."[17]

Some say every culture makes its own rules for what is right and what is wrong. Perhaps the most popular spiritual metaphor of the 20th Century is the relativist claim that "There are many paths, but all lead to the top of the mountain."

The relativists have practiced little mountain-climbing, I think. On real mountains, there is usually only one path to the summit. Other trails go part-way up. Then invariably the trail forks, and you have to choose — up or down. The same is true on Mount Tai. The trail along the summit ridge forks towards a Soviet-style weather station where hikers spend the night. Only one trail goes past Han Wu Di's monument to the summit.

The ancient Chinese sages could see for themselves that not all people go the same direction in life. The "Book of the Moral Way," the Taoist classic *Dao De Jing*, warned that though the Way wasn't hard to find, most people got lost in the woods spiritually:

"The great way is easy, yet people prefer by-paths
The court is corrupt,
The fields are overgrown with weeds
The granaries are empty;
Yet there are those dressed in fineries,
With swords at their sides,
Filled with food and drink
And possessed of too much wealth.
This is known as taking the lead in robbery.
Far indeed is this from the Way."[18]

To the men who mapped it, true goodness wasn't a "social contract," a covenant that evolved out of the community's needs. The Way existed before all things. A person's success in life depended on finding this one path. Even a person who found the *Tao* on his death-bed "has not lived in vain."[19]

忠 For three thousand years, the center lane of the Chinese moral
孝 highway has been an idea called *Zhong Xiao*.

What is *Xiao*? Dictionaries often translate it as "filial piety." We taste its flavor better in words like "faithfulness," "obedience" and "fidelity." *Xiao* is what children should feel for their parents. It is the obligation of the young to the old, of those protected to those who protect, of student to teacher.

The importance of *Zhong-Xiao* is expressed in a thousand scenes in China: A hanging at a New Year's festival. "To establish character and do what is right *Xiao* must come first." A sticker pasted to a telephone pole on a mountain road. "Of a thousand virtues *Xiao* is best, of ten thousand vices infidelity is greatest." Tribal girls at a railroad station dressed their best to go into town and buy a present for teacher. Flames sweeping a hill in Fujian Province covered with colored paper like autumn leaves as monks burn money for the dead. A science professor on a bus to Confucius' hometown: "Chinese need at the very least to do this much. Chinese talk about this word the most, but find it difficult to do."

But for three millenia in China, the ultimate expression of true loyalty in China came at the top of Mt. Tai.

The Three Hikers

The three famous leaders who used Tai as a pulpit probably influenced Chinese morality more than anyone. The first came as a follower of the Way. The other two set out to find their own paths to unity with the Ultimate.

These three hikers became the founders of spiritual dynasties. Not a single vendor, tour operator, farmer, or tourist on Mount Tai or anywhere else in China has gone untouched by what these three men thought and did.

In different ways, each prepared China for the one who would guide mankind back up the mountain into the presence of our Creator.

Yellow Mountain and rhododendrons in spring, Anhui Province.

Chapter Three

The Teacher And The Tyrant

A good way to stir a conversation in China is to bring up the name of Confucius.

The final section of the poll I took in mainland China asked for opinions on various religions. What do you think of Buddhism? Islam? Taoism? Forty years of materialist education had obviously had an effect: "I don't know" and "No opinion" were probably the most common responses.

But in response to the next question, "What do you think of Confucius?" most people gave quick and emotional responses.

"Oh! One of the world's great thinkers," said an old man who'd been imprisoned for his politics for twenty years. "The middle path is the best way—very scientific." A simple young woman with little education: "Confucius had a good influence on us." A college student and clothing manufacturer: "A milestone in the development of Chinese culture."

Most folk in Taiwan seemed to feel the same.*

For some in mainland China, though, the question stirred up a flicker of anger. "He was the most influential figure in Chinese culture, yet he also imprisoned Chinese culture," wrote one. "He shouldn't have discriminated against women," wrote a girl in Shanghai. He wasn't "resolute" enough, said someone else.

*(In response to somewhat different questions.)

25

In the southwest city of Kunming, at a park called Green Lake, huge flocks of seagulls from Lake Baikal in Siberia winter. By the spot where opportunistic gulls circle to catch bread crumbs from human visitors, every Thursday night young men and women gather to practice English. Also opportunistic, these students gather three deep around tourists from the hotel across the street not only for a morsel or two of English grammar, but to glean fresh perspectives on politics, literature, food, or the meaning of life, in English, Chinese, or even Japanese. The conversation often gets quite lively.

Once on a visit to this park a young woman told me she preferred Lao Tse to Confucius. I was surprised. Westerners often take the founder of Taoism to heart for his urbane, skeptical wit. But in China? Confucius seemed much more popular in my poll. Could it be that the clever Lao Tze would be closer to the hearts of this more intellectual young crowd? Might young intellectuals, after forty years of hearing Confucius was a reactionary, (Marxist for "fuddy-duddy") be embarrassed to stick up for this icon of traditional China?

So I took a fresh poll of the faces around me in the dark. "Whom do you prefer, *Kong Fu Zi* or Lao Tse?" The overwhelming, enthusiastic reply from these bright young Chinese: Confucius.

Not just their words, but their very presence showed that the spell China's "first teacher" cast upon China had not been broken.

How did he do it? What is the key to this cautious scholar's enduring popularity? How did it survive forty years of communist hostility?

Actually, the ideals of China's "First Teacher" had to endure a challenge every bit as fierce as Marxism while they were still young— the enmity of China's "First Emperor," the infamous tyrant Qin Shi Huang, who climbed Mount Tai some three hundred years after Confucius. No two men in ancient China were more different, and no two men played a greater role in forming China into what it is today.

Many people look on Confucianism and Christianity as rivals. As we look at what China's greatest thinker thought, saw, said and did, we will see that this is not the case. In fact it was the teachings of Marx that were foreign to China—which is not to say there was nothing of value in them. But Confucius was no more a rival to Jesus than moonlight is to sunshine, or a February plum blossom is to spring. In China's First Teacher came an echo or foreshadowing of the teacher yet to come. At the same time, we will see that Jesus also felt this anger many Chinese feel, and what's more, he knew what to do with it. Qin's Great Wall and equally magnificent tomb in quite different but dramatic ways are also parables of the life of Jesus, as we will see in the final section of the book.

The World Is Small

The land east of Mount Tai is a plain, planted mostly in corn. The "Golden Thread of the Yellow River" glistens forty miles to the north. The Yellow Sea beats the Shandong coast two hundred miles to the east. The sprawling grey provincial capital, Jinan, lies north along the rail line to Beijing. A few train stops south, in a cedar forest at the edge of a town called Qifu, rest the earthly remains of Confucius.

Confucius' greatest disciple, Mencius lived just a few miles away two hundreds years later. It was he who recorded Confucius' famous reflection on a visit to the mountain: "When you climb Mount Tai, *Xiao Tian Xia*—the world becomes small."

The grave of Confucius.

The world look small from the top of a mountain, if you look up. The horizon melts away, and the sky seems to grow.

When we follow Confucius' example by looking up, the world can look smaller than ever, thanks to telescopes. A modern Chinese writer says if the sun were an apple in Nanjing, the earth would be a chestnut ten kilometers away. The nearest star, he went on, would lie near Canton a thousand miles off.[1] Even that understates the discoveries of modern astronomy. To accurately scale the trillions of stars in the night sky to even a radish-sized earth, we'd need a model bigger than the planet. No wonder Albert Einstein said he understood only two to three percent of how the universe works.

The Chinese poet wrote that a "perfect man" looked up, "Saw the blue sky, and feared." In China, as in Israel, vision and humility were linked. In both nations, it was the teacher who climbed the path of *Xiao* highest, who saw furthest in every direction: towards Heaven, towards earth, in the direction of the far horizon, and into his own soul.

Humility Looks Down

One characteristic of the humble is they notice ordinary people. A humble person does what he can to help those in need, without allowing social differences to mar true friendship.

Kindness towards inferiors was not a common attitude in Confucius' day. Kings murdered to steal wives or even for target practice. The prevailing sentiment was that the best purpose a subject could serve was to die for his lord.

Confucius taught that the first duty of a king was to care for the common folk, though.

> "On becoming his steward, Yuan Ssu was given nine hundred measures of grain which he declined. The Master said, 'Can you not find a use for it in helping the people in your neighborhood?" [2]

Love, *Ren*, was the heart of Confucius' political philosophy. But he wasn't one who "sends a message" to the ruling class or a few coins to the needy, then goes home and locks the door. He welcomed poor students, encouraging them that if their hearts were "Set on the Way," to not be ashamed of poverty.[3] "In . . . the using of one's elbow for a pillow, joy is to be found."

Humility: To Know Thyself

Confucius was aware of his own faults and limitations, and he listened to criticism. "The gentleman. . . goes to men possessed by the Way to be put right," he said. [4] He dryly remarked on his fortune as a teacher himself because "Whenever I make a mistake, other people are sure to notice it." He saw himself not as a "benevolent man" or a "sage," but only as one who "learns without giving up" and "teaches without getting tired." The words "I don't know" loom large in the *Analects*.

Yet he never compromised his sense of dignity as a human being, or denied the special gifts bestowed on him. He was a teacher. He audaciously insisted that China conform to his lessons: that rulers learn kindness, and subjects dignity.

Confucius believed Heaven entrusted him with a two-fold mission: to preserve the best of China's traditions, and to teach true benevolence. Sometimes his driving sense of purpose prompted him to say things which sounded very immodest. Once, surrounded by enemies, he asked his disciples: "What can they do to me? God has chosen me to save this culture."

But if humility means to see things as they truly are, we can only ask, how did he know? He lived through the siege, and thanks to his survival, much of the best in ancient China was passed on. Confucius seemed to objectively view himself from a perspective that transcended the confines of his time.

Eager To Learn

The humble also take an interest in the world around them: people, nature, hobbies, a cause. They risk dignity or safety to read the bumpersticker on the car ahead, taste honey from a wild bee hive, or see if an experimental aircraft will fly. A humble person is too curious to be a slave to fear or reputation.

The world was small, but Confucius took an uncommon interest in everything on it. Go to any village, he said, and you might find someone kinder or more trustworthy than him, but you wouldn't find anyone more "eager to learn."[5] Like an absent-minded professor, he said he "forgets to eat when he tries to solve a problem" and even "forgets his worries and does not notice the onset of old age."[6]

Two passages show Confucius at moments of self-forgetful glee:

"Startled, the bird rose up and circled round before alighting. He said, 'The female pheasant on the mountain ridge, how timely her action is, how timely her action is!' Tzu-lu cupped one hand in the other in a gesture of respect towards the bird which, flapping its wings three times, flew away." [7]

"The Master heard the shao in Ch'i and for three months did not notice the taste of the meat he ate. He said, 'I never dreamt that the joys of music could reach such heights.'" [8]

Gazing At Heaven

Whether in friendship, or from the peak of Mount Tai, Confucius looked up, too. He paid respect to those whose wisdom, abilities and position exceeded his own. He avoided flattery. But even when he saw a man's faults, he knew how to pay a heart-felt compliment.

Confucius encouraged his disciples to speak of God with the deepest reverence of all.

"The gentleman stands in awe of three things. He is in awe of the Decree of Heaven. He is in awe of great men. He is in awe of the words of the sages. The small man, being ignorant of the Decree of Heaven, does not stand in awe of it. He treats great men with insolence and the words of the sages with derision."[9]

"When you have offended against Heaven, there is nowhere you can turn to in your prayers." [10]

But on this subject the humblest words Confucius spoke were, again, "I don't know."

"Someone asked about the *ti (Di)* sacrifice. The Master said, 'It is not something I understand, for whoever understands it will be able to manage the Empire as easily as if he had it here,' pointing to his palm." [11]

It is a measure of the greatness of Confucius that he knew his limits, yet did not impose them on others. He did not know how to approach Heaven. But looking across the centuries, he saw that someone else might.

Confucius' Greatest Hope

Later disciples often called Confucius a *sheng ren*, a "holy man." (The word is usually translated "sage.") It was not mere politeness that caused him to decline the title: he was a man who took words seriously. "How dare I call myself a holy man?" He asked.

One aspect of Confucius' ideal was self-sacrifice. A good man, he taught, would even be willing to "accept death" to "accomplish benevolence." Moral excellence was not something to be taken lightly.

Who deserved to be called holy? Someone asked the teacher if a hypothetical hero who "Brought help to the multitude" would qualify. Confucius considered this vague question carefully; it seemed to stir some grand, heroic vision of his own. Even Yao and Shun, he concluded, naming two legendary Chinese rulers, could probably not do such good that they would earn such a lofty title in his eyes.

Confucian scholar Chen Jingpan described what Confucius' was looking for:

> "A Sage would have transcended the achievements of any living being which had so far existed. He was thought of as being in the same category as the Divine Being of whom the Superior Man should always stand in awe. He is, in short, the ideal of the ideal human life, and the highest standard for human beings."[12]

Professor Chen said Confucius' ideal man would benefit "all the people of the world." Chen described him as a "Savior of the World."[13] Confucius, looking out toward the East Asian coast of 600 B.C., believed such a person had yet to be born.

From the day Confucius stood at the summit of Mount Tai to this, many have tried their hand at being "Savior of the World." Few who took on this enterprise matched the humble character or followed such humane and sensible ideas as Confucius taught. But let me amend the question Confucius' disciples asked him. What if one humble man did manage to bring all the world hope? What if he brought people in every country to a point where they could not only see the world better, but peer into Heaven? What if he brought salvation not by conquest or propaganda, but—as Confucius hinted—by self-sacrifice?

As we will see, at the same time on the other side of the world another nation was also awaiting a Savior. Like China, this nation was also a Middle Kingdom—made central not by the union of three teachings, as China, but by the union of three continents and the spiritual history of the human race.

Confucius never said the Savior would be Chinese.

Confucius' Children

Kong Fu Zi sought political power most of his life. He never attained high rank. No doubt at his death many thought his story had come to an end.

In the next few centuries several great thinkers followed in his footsteps: Mozi, Mencius, Xun Zu, Lao Zi, Zhuang Zi. They discussed the love of God, the nature of man, freedom, duty, and death, often with wit and insight.

Many of Confucius' disciples and rivals seemed to accomplish more than the First Teacher. They tutored kings, founded Taoism and other brilliant movements, and made quick marks on Chinese history. One even invented supply-side economics.

But none saw as far as Confucius. Few saw well enough to say "I don't see."

Instead, an easy certainty about the past and the other world crept in. Arguments became breezy and superficial, people exaggerating differences, as if afraid to find anything worthwhile in an opponent's ideas.

Confucius' children went their separate ways, each taking much of value with him. But China lost more than the sum of the parts: the vision that comes from humility was often lost.

A Tyrant Climbs Mount Tai

Then a man appeared who seemed to get more done than all scribblers and preachers combined. He turned everything Confucius taught on its head. Arrogance was his path to glory. One measure of his success is the fact that the word "China" is derived from his family name, Qin. (Pronounced like the English word "chin.")

Qin Shi Huang, "Qin, the First Emperor" united China after centuries of feudal rivalry. He created a new system of government, abolishing the aristocracy and setting up the famous exam system for government service. He built the Great Wall.

A missionary of the last century wrote that Napoleon was "not even in the same class" as Qin.

"Chin had no gattling guns, men of war, powder or steam, but for soaring ambition, never was there a head or heart on this planet, before or since, that was possessed of a greater amount." [14]

Yet Chinese historians depict the First Emperor as petty, clownish and vain. They tell how, when he met bandits on a trip, he halted all the machinery of state for ten days to hunt them. He sent thousands of young men and women to look for the "islands of the immortals." He murdered those who dared disprove of his antics. Two officials complained, from a safe distance:

"The emperor never learns of his mistakes and hence grows daily more arrogant, while his underlings, prostrate with fear, flatter and deceive him in order to curry favor." [15]

Like Confucius, Emperor Qin took nature outings. When he climbed China's holy mountains, however, he neither "Looked up and feared" nor looked out and learned. For him, a mountain was a pedestal, a stage on which to show off. He set commemorative stones on the summits of his conquests:

> "The August Emperor mounted the throne, issuing edicts, clarifying laws, which his subjects observe and obey. In the twenty-sixth year of his rule he first united the world; there were none who did not come to him in submission."[16]

Qin expected the mountains and the clouds to submit to him too. Once, when it rained during a climbing trip, to avenge himself on the goddess of the mountain, he had all the trees cut down.

In 219 B.C. Emperor Qin came to the newly-conquered kingdom of Lu. He climbed Mount Tai.

But the Emperor got rained out again. He fled the summit, and waited out the storm under a pine tree lower down. In a typically clownish but unusually generous act of conciliation, he promoted the tree under which he huddled to "fifth rank counselor."

Why did Qin climb Mount Tai? It is said he was looking for herbs to make him immortal.

One way to say "die" in Chinese is to "see God." Despite the fact that he climbed the mountain where God was worshiped, Emperor Qin was not eager for this meeting. He spent much of his life hunting the elixir of youth. He forbade ministers to mention death in his presence. He must have realized the futility of trying to escape though. All the while his craftsmen dug, carved and molded the most magnificent tomb on earth. Portions of this tomb have been opened to tourists near the city of Xian and become one of the great marvels of China.

The Teacher And The Tyrant

Emperor Qin left China a wall, a tomb and a name. The structure of Chinese government and the Chinese written language remain impressed with his imperial stamp to this day. But few admire his governing style or character.

A girl touches a stove, and learns what "fire" means. In the same way, Emperor Qin taught China the meaning of the word "tyrant." China drew back. After his death, official China fled to the political philosophy of Confucius: kindly government, rule by tacit consent of the people, and the duty of kings to conform to the will of a loving Heaven.

The lesson stuck. Even two thousand years later, Chinese Marxists posed as teachers to "re-educate" China, rather than relying on frank terror so often as the Russian Marxists. And the one period when they employed terror the most, was preceded by ferocious attacks on Confucius. But now, Confucius is popular in China again.

The First Teacher gave China two things of great value besides this ideal of kindly government. The Chinese word "teach"教 represents the fusion of two characters: *Xiao*, 孝 humble loyalty, and *Wen*, 文 culture, which is part of Chinese words for "civilization," "literature," and "written word." These two ancient values, humility and love of writing, are also the heritage Confucius helped create and preserve. They are linked. Learning and reading both involve a kind of submission. Perhaps that is why Qin was also a great burner of books.

"Oh My Father, Who Begot Me!"

I got to know a young man when I first lived in Hong Kong who spoke excellent English. His dream, he told me, was to "become an American yuppie."

My friend showed little patience with one aspect of American culture, though: old folks' homes. "You Westerners will never understand." He said. "Our parents take care of us when we're small. We take care of them when they're old."

His sentiments dated at least to the *Book of Poetry*, which was said to have been edited by Confucius:

"Oh my father, who begot me!
Oh my mother, who nourished me!
Ye indulged me, ye fed me,
Ye helped me up, ye supported me,
Ye looked after me, ye never left me,
Out and in ye bore me in your arms.
If I would return your kindness
It is like great Heaven, illimitable."[17]

Confucius served as a bridge for such sentiments from ancient to modern China. One scholar wrote of him,

"Filial piety is the alpha and omega of his ethics. It includes and logically presupposes every other virtue under heaven. Thus, honesty, justice, courage, self-control, modesty and loyalty, all come under the single rubric of devotion to parents."[18]

A young professional friend in Hong Kong gave seventy percent of her income to her mother. By contrast, the stereotype of the grateless American child who sends his parents to the old folks' home provides a foil against which Chinese moralists still spar. *Xiao* is both social security for parents, and the rallying cry of a civilization. As the professor on the bus to Confucius' birthplace told me, "Chinese talk about this the most."

A rural classroom in Guizhou Province.

"First Teacher"

Confucius also infected China with his passion for learning. In Taiwan, his vision was funneled and channeled by what is called the "stuff the duck" method of education.

An American studied for a year at a graduate school in Taiwan. In that year, he studied harder than ever before in his life. But after a year he was asked to leave. Why? He wasn't sure. One day on a return visit he met the president of the school, Dr. L, in an elevator. Here, he thought, was his chance to get an answer. It was a small institution, and he felt sure the educator would remember him.

"Could you tell me what the problem was last year?" he asked.

Dr. L peered at the student through thick glasses. "We're very happy with the way you've been studying." He frowned. "It was that other American. He was lazy."

The elevator stopped and Dr. L got off.

It suddenly dawned on the student what had happened.

Dr. L was near-sighted, and had mistaken him for the good student. The incident triggered reflections. Why did so many teachers and students at the institute, and in most colleges in Taiwan, also wear glasses? Why had his own eyes also begin twitching after a year of trying to keep up there?

"Stuff the duck" education consists of memorizing a huge mass of facts spoon-fed by teachers, until the brain (and the eyes) are full.

Taiwan has risen to a high rank in the world of commerce and technology by concentrating on small objects: equations, computer chips, financial tables. For those who spend their days looking at things close up, it sometimes becomes hard to see things at a distance.

City lights drown out stars, though stars are far brighter. In the same way, in prosperous countries, the multiple details involved in making a living may distract us from seriously look at life itself. Of Taiwan's thousands of gods many ask no more than correct lottery numbers. Many Americans use the gift of literacy for no greater purpose than to read the t.v. guide.

In mainland China, poverty and repression have produced many with a deep hunger to learn, like Confucius.

The government "stuffs the ducks" with Marxist ideology, and little else. A brilliant mathematician who made about thirty dollars a month told me, "The government hates intellectuals."

Would Confucius stand out as especially "eager to learn" at an English corner? Many Chinese today, like him, ask hard questions, expect honest answers, and tell you what they think. The party might as well try to cram a flock of phoenix in a chicken coop, as try to squeeze the intellectual hunger from this generation of mainland Chinese.

Thanks in part to Confucius. But why for some in China does mention of a humble man who taught kindness spark anger?

The third man who climbed Mount Tai became a teacher who channeled China's anger to make himself her tyrant. His name was Mao Tse Tung.

Red Army soldier, Sichuan Province.

Chapter Four

The Tao Of Revolution

It was an attractive cottage. Two stories, a bright red gate for the family car, with ferns well-spaced along a shiny tiled balcony, it breathed good taste. Behind it, bamboo waved on a lush green ridge. In front lay a sun-drenched plain of papaya trees and sugar cane. The village stretched along a road that marked the half-way point between the mountains and a white line of surf to the east. Most houses in the Tairoko tribal village, by contrast to the surrounding beauty, were of mildewy concrete. But here and there arose other nice new homes.

The pastor's wife at a run-down Presbyterian church across the street told me how this house was built. "'Mei Lan' used to come to church," she said. "My daughter and she were good friends. She especially liked to sing the songs. Then her mother asked her if she'd mind quitting school. 'How about working in a factory in Taipei?'"

I'd seen "factories" in Taipei's "Snake Alley" where tribal girls worked. Barred windows glowed pink in dark alleys. Teenage girls beckoned to a dark crowd of men that filled the alleyways every night.

A scar-faced man who worked in one of those houses later told me he beat a girl with a brick when she didn't meet her "quota." She'd slept with fewer than thirty men that day.

Some pimps found an even better weapon to keep girls in line: the word *Xiao*.

A sick mother needed medicine. A little brother needed tuition. A father owed a gambling or whiskey debt. The family had its sights set on a rich sugar cane field or a new house.

It'd be "*Not-Xiao*," disloyal, to let them down.

The lights were off, and I was denied a look at the father and mother who sold their little girl to all comers in an urban hell-hole to build this new house. That night, I couldn't sleep, and went outside to watch the stars.

Another young Tairoko man, once a pimp himself, told me many of the girls he knew as a young man are dead now. (And that was before AIDS.) During a visit to his village twenty miles to the south, he pointed an eighteen-year-old neighbor out to me. She sat outside her house and stared like an old woman in a nursing home, while her mother rocked her baby.

This man took a house-to-house survey of the area. He found one Tairoko girl in five had been sold into prostitution. I met a girl from one of the villages he surveyed whose three older sisters had all been sold. It seemed she was next on the block.

What Are Women Good For?

I mentioned earlier the anger some Chinese feel towards Confucius. The girl in Shanghai, who complained that he "discriminated" against women, flared up when I mentioned the concept of *Xiao*. "My mother and I often argue about this," she said. "The old Chinese idea was 'If the father wants the son to die, the son should die.' She thinks that way too."

She went on to tell me:

"Do you know what a *shuyu* is? She's a kind of prostitute — not an ordinary *jinu*, but someone who has some culture, an educated person.

"There once was a *shuyu* named Du Shi Liang. She met a man named Li Jia, and they fell in love. But his parents felt families should marry at their own level (*men dang hu dui*), and opposed the marriage. It would be 'Not Xiao' to marry her. So he sold her to a merchant. She jumped into a river and killed herself.

"According to the society of that day, Li Jia did the right thing. But it was a tragic end for Du Shi Liang. China has a lot of stories like that."

Jung Chang related several similarly tragic true stories in her family biography, *Wild Swans*. Her great-grandfather gave her grandmother as concubine to a Beijing general. Her grandmother, a girl named Yu Fang, "hated" the idea of becoming a concubine. But to argue would be "unfilial."

> ". . . and to be unfilial was tantamount to treason. . . The only way to say no and be taken seriously was to commit suicide."[1]

Yu Fang became mistress or prisoner of a mansion in Manchuria while her husband lived in Beijing. Short of the story-book solution of killing herself, all she could do was complain. Her father didn't sympathize.

> "A good woman was not supposed to have a point of view at all, and if she did, she certainly should not be so brazen as to talk about it. He would quote the Chinese saying, 'If you are married to a chicken, obey the chicken; if you are married to a dog, obey the dog.'"[2]

A house that prostitution built, Hualien, Taiwan.

41

Others in her circle fared even worse. In a friend's family, two concubines drugged the wife's food and that of a male servant, and put the two in bed together. When the husband came home and found them, he locked his wife in a room until she went mad. Yu Fang's mother prayed for her next incarnation, "Let me become a cat or a dog, but not a woman."

A happy family life is the cornerstone of Chinese morality. Yet, it would have been hard to find anyone who found much peace in many traditional Chinese upper-class families besides the animal at the front gate. The first wife had to live with her husband's other women. They were usually at her mercy. Children grew up confused—you meet some in Hong Kong who are still reaping a harvest of pain from their fragmented childhood. Poor men had a choice of celibacy or prostitutes. Many poor women, like Mei Lan, had no choices at all.

So much misery for the pleasure of one man. As for him, did the pleasures of patriarchy really compensate for living in a hornets' nest?

Why Rivers Overrun Their Banks

From the summit of Mount Tai on a clear day you can see the "Golden Ribbon of the Yellow River." Early Chinese civilization grew like a willow along the banks of this great stream. Despite periodic flooding, the Yellow River nourished China, fed crops, carried away trash, and moved produce.

The *Tao* is China's Yellow River of the heart. Like the river, the ideal of loyal submission enriches a whole society. But also like the river, it can corrode, too.

This is why China doesn't always need obedient sons.

Four times in the last century and a half, young Chinese had enough of submission. They threw down plows, abandoned fields and textbooks, said goodbye to parents. They braved wild animals, hostile tribesmen, and hunger, as well as government troops armed to the teeth. Why? Loyalty had been pushed to the edge. They had been trampled on by those with power too many times.

The most successful of China's modern rebels first climbed Mount Tai in 1919.

The last Qing ruler, the Empress Dowager, who had ruled until just a few years before, considered herself a disciple of the Chinese sages. Yet as a Manchurian, she discriminated against ethnic Chinese. Corrupt and incompetent, while she patronizingly quoted Confucius to her subjects, foreigners gobbled up China bite-by-bite. Even her fit of temper against the West during the Boxer Rebellion accomplished nothing but more misery for China.

North of Mt. Tai, the city of Shanghai was now occupied by foreigner G.I.s. Beggars stumbled through the streets, while the rich escorted ladies in minks. Some of the cream of China's young manhood lined gutters, waiting for a fix of opium. Others who could have cared for their children, waited in cubicles for drunk businessmen.

Something had gone wrong with China's "family values."

An English woman I know who works with drug addicts in Hong Kong wrote of "Greedy black-mailing mothers" who hindered recovery by caring more for their own selfish whims than for the lives of their sons.[3] Over two and a half millennia, the lines of authority drawn by Confucius became set in stone, even in families where the love that should have softened them was lacking.

Was Confucius to blame?

Chen Jingpan denies Confucius was at fault for the spin later generations put on the ideal of *Xiao:*

"Family despotism, with all the evils resulting from it, such as the belief that 'if a father wants his son to die, the so cannot do otherwise but to go to die,' is really a later development of Confucianism. . . And is not in accordance with the spirit of Confucius himself and his earliest disciples."[4]

Confucius did teach, however, that a good son makes no change in his fathers' way of life for three years. Confucius also said even if his parents were in the wrong, a child should "Never fail to comply."

Confucius did his best to channel China's traditional values in a life-giving direction. He cared more for virtue than for pleasure, and seldom took his pleasures at the expense of others. Many "great teachers" both in China and the West have done much worse. Yet still the river floods.

In the *Analects*, you find a few comments like "I've never met a man who cared more for virtue than for beautiful women," and a record that Confucius gave a daughter and two nieces in marriage to men he admired. Other than that, he seldom noticed women. He only had one wife, and never talked about her. His students were all men. Lessons seldom touched on relations between the sexes.

Husbands need something stronger than silence. We need a teacher who sets an example, not only how to love and respect the old, but how to love and respect women—who cares for virtue *in* women.

Zhong Xiao As A Weapon Of War

As Japanese troops swarmed across China in 1932, the Ministry of Education in Tokyo insisted all schools in Japan install shrines with portraits of the emperor. A teacher at a Christian school, Takaaki Aikawa, guarded his school shrine in the twilight hours:

"Four times during the night I had to go see that all was well. . . I dared not neglect my patrol since I had often heard that principles of public schools had committed suicide because of some damage done to the Imperial Portraits."[5]

Mr. Aikawa avoided buses that led past the emperor's palace. "Kyujo-yokai," worship of the palace, had become the new duty of patriotic Japanese. The secret police arrested those who didn't bow low enough as they went by.

Qin Shi Huang was the first ruler to call himself "*Huang Di*," taking the name of God as part of his title. Later, Taoist priests said there were five *Di*s, of whom the Jade Emperor was mightiest. Meanwhile, on earth, many "Sons of Heaven" ruled like gods behind imperial walls.

Confucius spoke of the need to "rectify names." He understood that to each role a kind and degree of authority is proper, and misdirected loyalty can be deadly. A rose may smell the same by any name, but if you label it "digitalis" and sell it as heart medicine, sick people die. And those who survive look with suspicion at all medicine.

It is told how once a swan chick grew up in a duck's nest. Later he learned that the bird who posed as his mother was an imposter. He set out through the farmyard in a daze asking chickens and geese, "Are you my mother?"

Human nature yearns for God. Even the most atheistic ideology can only disguise or pervert this drive. Recent mass suicides and murders by cults in Tokyo, Texas and Switzerland, are extreme examples of what happens when people set the wrong altar on Mount Tai. Confucius seemed to see this danger. He taught China to be cautious yet not cynical, to weigh answers with sobriety, and to look before we leap. He showed the humility of the "Way of Heaven" by his manner. History shows what happens when those who pose as teachers ignore these lessons.

But one thing Confucius lacked: closeness to the Father. China still felt orphaned, and kept looking for Someone to worship—often in dangerous places.

Traveler's Checks For The Dead

One place many looked was among the dead.

According to my poll, most Taiwanese believe in evil spirits. One of my students in Japan, a vivacious, worldly young woman, was petrified by an experience with a spirit at a hotel in Tokyo. I've had many other students and friends in both countries who've had similar experiences.

I noted before Chinese feel the gods "Are there to be fooled." One way to fool spirits is to burn pieces of paper, sometimes blank or colored, sometimes printed with literally "hellacious" sums on the "Bank of Hades," to bribe keepers of the other world to care for dead ancestors.

But whom does this custom really fool? And who does the fooling?

The mother of an Ami friend fell ill. It was clear she was going to die. "I'm a Christian," she told her daughter. "After I die, don't burn paper for me."

The woman died. Her daughter met a witch. (A popular occupation in Taiwan.) The witch had never met her mother, but somehow spoke in a voice just like her mother's. "I'm so hungry!" it said. "Burn paper for me!" The witch became angry when she refused.

Sometime later my friend felt so depressed she decided to step in front of a car. (I learned firsthand in Taiwan how common suicidal impulses are among those who do business with spirits.) At that moment a stranger came up to her and told her, "Don't kill yourself. God loves you." She became a Christian.

What do you do if you don't believe in spirits, but at night your house shakes and invisible feet stomp across your hall? On my first visit to China, friends I was traveling with met a young woman with this problem. Atheist professors and Buddhist priests were unable to help her. She'd become a nervous wreck and lost many pounds. My friends prayed with her and both house and occupant found peace.

Most of the human race has always felt our planet was haunted. Science hasn't proven so sure a defense as many hoped. Is it any wonder that mankind feels a need for divine protection?

In regard to the occult, the example China's First Teacher set was incomplete. He steered clear of both gods and human demagogues — both sensible policies. But China as a whole has seldom been able to avoid either entirely. Mt. Tai became cluttered with idols, and the minds of the people with demeaning superstitions. Why? Because China knew her "Heavenly Parent" only from a far distance. Her wisest teacher, who felt an ideal father was distant from his son, also sensed no special closeness to God. He did not know how to bridge the gap between Heaven and earth, or fully understand why it needed to be bridged.

The East Is Red

From the top of Mt. Tai, Mao Tse Tung looked down on a dispirited land.

Communism gave traditionally sedentary scholars an
often-unwelcome chance to work with their hands.
Zhong Shan University, Canton.

Mao had guarded the works of the sages as a Beijing University
librarian. They'd proven as impotent as the Empress Dowager to save
China from humiliation. A western visitor pointed to those classics
and said China was "pining" for "another Qin:"

> "The libraries and brains of the literati are stuffed full of useless,
> literary rubbish — old, mouldy, unusable lumber and fit only
> to make a bonfire of."[6]

He suggested "We would not approve of burying the scholars alive,
head and all, but simply up to their necks."

The wine which the sages had laid away so carefully had soured
and turned to vinegar. The powerful used ideals to squash the
powerless. Like the Ami girl at the side of the road, the Chinese were
waiting for a Ruler who didn't just talk about loyalty to make people
obey, but earned it by showing his love.

In 1917, rebels came to power in Russia, angry at old values. Their
teachings fell on fertile soil in China. Mao Tse Tung, a young man who
often quarreled with his father, was one who listened eagerly.

Mao lit the "bonfire" that purified the Middle Kingdom. His Red
Army brought young Chinese freedom from fear of the dead. The

46

communists raised the status of women. They freed slaves, burnt opium, reformed prostitutes, and taught peasants to read. They built roads. They taught sanitation and health. They planted millions of trees, so almost every major city street in mainland China is shaded.

Mao burnt the books of the literati, too: the *Analects*, the *Mencius*, the *Book of Changes*, the *Lotus*, the *Bible*. He also buried scholars to their necks—and beyond.

First he buried them in slogans. For forty years every radio and television broadcast, textbook, office and factory, almost every page of every newspaper, drilled the nation in revolution. Like the Buddhist vision of a billion tiny Buddhas equally distributed through time and space, Mao's thoughts covered every blank wall.

"Sailing on the seas depends on the helmsman,
All things on earth depend on the sun
Moistened by rain and dew, young crops grow strong,
To make revolution, we must rely on Mao Tse Dong thought."[7]

China learned to look to the future instead of the past, to care for children more than ancestors, to seek answers from science rather than shamans.

What was the heart of Chairman Mao's thinking? He returned to Mt Tai to spell it out clearly.

In the morning, as the sun rises from China's eastern seaboard, it filters through a mist. Mao looked towards the sea and spoke a three word antithesis to Confucius' three-word thesis: *Dong Fang Hong*. "The east is red."

It was a clever choice of words. Mao's name, Dong, means "east." Mao had led the Red Army to victory in the east. He had cleansed China by the blood of her oppressors.

But to be clever is not always to be wise.

Confucius looked up and saw Heaven. Mao looked down, and like Qin, saw only the shadow of his own success. The east is red: I have conquered, China has "changed color." But like Qin, Mao was fooled. Morning mists don't last, and neither did his social engineering schemes.

The peak of Mao's red tide came a few years later.

In 1966, a time of new thinking around the world, Mao stood on a rostrum on the Gate of Heavenly Peace and preached his "new morality." "The wisdom of the revolution can defeat Heaven!" He shouted.

A popular song echoed off the capitals' stones:

"The hows and whys of Marxism,

Tens of thousands of lines and threads,
Come down in the last analysis
To one single sentence, which is:
To rebel is justified!"[8]

China's propagandists made the same point in many ways. Confucius was an "advocate of reaction." The suppression of old by new was the "eternal and inviolable law of the universe." True communists would always oppose "conservatism, restoration and retrogression" and fight for "change, revolution and social progress." No force on earth could "obstruct the forward movement of history." [9]

A Freudian slip from the summit of Tai Shan. A graffitiist, no doubt a Red Guard, has scrawled "Chairman Mao" (Mao Zhu Xi) on this rock at the top. Only "Mao Zhu" — "Lord Mao" — is now visible.

No village in China was untouched by this message. Temples, mosques and churches were torn down. Priests were tried before mobs —even some who worked for the secret police. Leaders of the communist party were tortured in a prison near Beijing until many committed suicide. Scholars were literally buried up to their necks in farm mud. Some had to wade through human waste every day at forced labor.

The east became redder still when the spirit of rebellion turned in on itself.

At the university where I later studied, students confiscated guns and artillery from an army base and fought a mob from a factory. I'm told three hundred people were killed.

Another "reactionary" who died was the husband of my English teacher. It had been a love marriage, and the two often walked hand-in-hand on campus. But it seems he was a counter-revolutionary. Red Guards threw him off the upper floor of a campus building.

On the other end of China, in the town of Shi Gu, "Stone Drum", stood the drum for which the town was named. This beautiful village was built at a ford on the banks of the first bend in the Yangtze River after it flows down from Tibet. Legend warned that if the drum were ever broken, disaster would come on China. In a typical act of defiance, Red Guards broke the drum.

Like that drum, many lives around China were shattered by the disaster that was the Cultural Revolution.

In China you are likely to meet old intellectuals who spent the prime of their lives slopping pigs and being paraded through streets with dunce caps on their heads. You'll meet middle-aged men and women who spent youths shouting slogans; playing at the easy work of tearing apart, rather than learning to build. Another of my teachers, a man of Red Guard age who taught Chinese conversation, could hardly speak standard Chinese himself.

Yet many feel Mao was right about one thing: sometimes, to rebel is justified.

In the spring of 1989, some who learned this lesson gathered again beneath Tiananmen Gate. They demanded freedom, an end to corruption, and better living standards. China's rulers granted the leaders an interview. A 20-year-old named Wu Er Kai Xi publicly scolded Prime Minister Li Peng for not getting to the meeting on time.

I was in Taiwan at the time. Somehow I felt the old Confucian leadership on that island was more shocked at Wu's boldness than the communists. Deng Xiao Ping had seen students criticize leaders before. He'd heard the roar of the crowd before. He may have had flashbacks from the Cultural Revolution: he was on a platform. Students were beating him. A mob screamed for blood. And so, in a crack of guns and a roar of tanks, his Party served notice: to rebel was no longer justified.

Many look back on both rebellious eras with honest nostalgia. People believed in something then. The Red Guards didn't know their leaders were manipulating them as badly as any Confucian-quoting Son or Daughter of Heaven. Nor did they know that Mao, with private pools, villas scattered across China, and dozens of young girls at his beck and call, had become chief among hypocrites.

The world has turned, and revolution come full circle. As in 1919, few trust a man in uniform in today's China. Girls are tricked and sold into prostitution in Thailand along China's southern border. AIDS is spreading in from Burma, and brothels have sprung up across China. Families are threatened by a rising divorce rate and the growing influence of "Western" sexual mores.

Which should China choose; the Way of Loyalty, or the Way of Rebellion?

She needs both. Not just two teachers who attract two different kinds of people. She needs a sage who binds disparate strands of morality into a single thread and joins broken fragments of truth. China is looking for a leader, humble and kind like Confucius and with his integrity. She also needs a general who is bold enough to reach for Heaven: a man with fire in his soul. Somebody who stands against oppressors and says, "Love the weak or face the wrath of God."

The ancient realist Hsun Tzu wrote of human nature,

> "Crooked wood needs to undergo steaming and bending by
> the carpenter's tools; then only is it straight."[10]

Two thousand years ago in Israel a carpenter opened shop—not to work wood or stone, but human hearts.

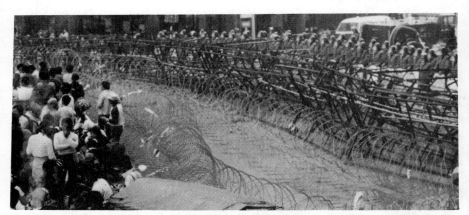

The Tao of revolution: confrontation between troops and demonstrators
for independance, Taipei, Taiwan.

Chapter Five

Son of Heaven

Their son was missing; somewhere he had slipped away from the tour group and was gone.

The anxious parents retraced their steps to the capital city. A day of searching showed up nothing. Finally, they came to the temple, where annual sacrifices to the Lord of Heaven were made. There they found him, deep in conversation with the priests.

Exasperated, his mother asked, "Don't you know your father and I have been looking all over for you?"

Frightened mothers often ask questions like that: rhetorical, even trick questions, but born of love. "How many times have I told you . . . ?" "Don't you know better than to. . . .?" The purpose is to make a point, not elicit information. You can't say "Yes" and you can't say "No." But you have to say something.

But this boy answered with a reply that stunned his parents. "Don't you understand I had to be doing my Father's work?"

What on earth did the child mean? There his father stood. He'd been worried sick, the same as his mother. Who was he talking about, his "father?" What business could this "father" have in the temple for a twelve year-old boy to do?

His mother never forgot this odd answer.

Twenty years passed. The son was back in the capital. The streets were alive with the rumor of more mysterious things he'd said. In his "father's" name, he told blind men to open their eyes and prostitutes that they were forgiven. He called respected religious figures "snakes."

51

His boldness prompted questions again, born of anger this time. "Your father? Who do you mean, your father? Who are you claiming to be?"

At his answer, men tore their clothes in protest. They seized and beat him. Then they nailed him to a beam of wood on a hill above the capital, and jeered at him as he died.

The young man, his body wracked by pain, looked down from the cross, seeing the angry crowd and the capital city spread below. He spotted his mother, and his closest friend standing nearby. "Dear woman," he told her. "Here is your son." And to the friend, "Here is your mother."[1]

****

The four records of the most famous man in history give only one picture of him as a child. That glimpse is a riddle: a boy who refused to go home so he could stay in his "Father's house."

The riddle grips us to the moment of his death. He died in a way that would have horrified Confucius: a first-born son publicly stripped and tortured as a criminal in front of his loving mother, leaving her no grandchildren. Yet he embraced that death in the name of his "Father." And even with pain pouring over him in waves, he reached out to touch her.

Does Jesus teach *Xiao*?

Like many questions people asked Jesus, this one is a trick. If the answer is "No," then Christianity denies the best moral sense of the Chinese people. If "Yes," how can Christians speak against tyrants who use *Xiao* to keep the weak in line? Yet just as a Carpenter needs a sharp blade to shape wood, so a teacher needs to make his points clear and unambiguous or they will do little to form his students.

But as Lao Tse and the Zen Buddhists showed, an answer that says both "yes" and "no" doesn't need to be contradictory or vague. It only needs to be a paradox.

Modern physics shows how a single substance can be defined by opposing qualities. Light, for example, is both particle and wave. Not only the ethic of Jesus, but his identity—humble Messiah, sinless convict, obedient rebel—binds together conflicting ideals. He took the submission of Confucius and the rebellion of Mao, magnified each a hundred times, and combined them into one truth, definite and dynamic as a beam of sunlight in his father's workshop after an afternoon of rain.

The Jewish Mount Tai

The Jewish view of right and wrong, like Confucianism, grew in a soil richly fertilized with the teachings of *xiao*. Confucius brought a vision of humility back from Mt. Tai. A thousand years previous, Moses carried a stone tablet carved with these words down from Mount Sinai:

"You must be *kabed* to your father and your mother, so you will live a long time in the land the Lord your God is giving you."[2]

The Hebrew word *kabed* carries four meanings, according to one commentator: (1) To prize highly. (2) To care for. (3) To show respect for. (4) To obey. [3] Rarely do words in two languages overlap so closely as *kabed* and *xiao*.

I once heard a Korean-American believer insult his father in public. Later he told me that as a Christian he no longer felt bound to "that old Confucian stuff" about respecting parents. But as I reminded him, "It's in the Bible, too."

The Old Testament took loyalty to the elderly seriously. The first four of the Ten Commandments were about respecting God. "Be *kabed* to your parents" was next, rating first mention among the rules which were to govern conduct between people.

Other passages drove the point home:

"Listen to your father who gave you birth, and don't look down on or despise your mother when she is old. . . Let your father and mother be glad; and she who bore you celebrate!"[4]

"Stand in the presence of a person with grey hair, honor the elderly and revere your God! I am the Lord."[5]

The Jewish Prophets And The Radical Left

But in the grain of Jewish Scripture were hidden germs of revolution, too. "Do not make for yourselves any carved image, of animals below, of the stars above. . . "[6] Some may think the idea of a Jealous God to be outdated or provincial. But the hostility of the Jewish prophets to "idolatry" was the most subversive concept in the ancient world. It sounded radical to Israel's neighbors, and when these teachings reached a China that had accustomed itself to lesser gods than *Huang Tian Shang Di*, it sounded just as radical. "Pluck the tablets off the family altar and throw them in the fire. Take a sledge hammer to all the gods on Mount Tai but one. Leave your idols of stick and stone and worship the One True God who made Heaven and Earth."

Each of China's modern "radical" movements contained a strand from the Jewish writings. The Tai Ping rebellion of the last century began when a Hakka man was handed a "Christian" tract whose content was based almost entirely on the sternest passages of the Old Testament.

Communism was invented by a Jew brought up as a Christian. Chiang Kai Shek's pastor once told me the old warlord's favorite part of the Bible were the battles of the Old Testament.

The prophets were dangerous men. Chinese civilization is one of many that have been overturned when people listened to just half of what they said.

But their message was radical in another sense, too. The word radical has to do with the roots of a thing, and the prophets call China back to one of its roots. What the emperor could do only once a year, they invited every man, woman and child on earth to join. In the quiet of a thatch hat, a peasant could meet *Shang Di*.

In the ancient world no one spoke with a clearer voice about obedience to God than the Jewish prophets—or in defense of the weak. Isaiah, Jeremiah, Amos and the others never stopped reminding Israel of its duty to orphans, widows, and strangers. "Do not profane the name of your God," they warned, by selling girls as prostitutes or abandoning the poor and weak. Those who did not listen, would face the judgement of Heaven.

The Jewish people assumed this message was for them alone. But their prophets spoke of a "Messiah" who like Confucius' "holy man" would one day bring a blessing to "far corners of the earth."[7] His authority would be absolute: the "increase of his government" would have "no end."[8] He would be called "Mighty God" and "Everlasting Father."[9] But he would exercise that authority on behalf of the weak. He would overthrow oppressors, and bring "good news to the poor" and "freedom for captives."[10] Salvation would come not from an unfeeling imperial bureaucracy or a distant Heaven, but by the "zeal" of the "Lord Almighty."[11] The prophets were also more specific than Confucius about where the world's Savior would be born: into a little town just south of the capital called Bethlehem.[12]

Paradox Found

The Gospels say Jesus cured the sick with a few simple words. "Pick up your mattress and go home!" He said to a crippled man, and the man was healed.[13] "Open!" He spoke into the ears of a deaf person, and the person heard.[14]

Did these things really happen? We'll consider the historical credibility of Jesus' miracles in a later chapter. But we can see for ourselves that Jesus mended the broken ideals of China with the same simple eloquence.

"Is it all right to divorce?" Someone asked. "He created them man and woman," Jesus answered, "What God has joined, let no man separate."[15] Like a stone thrown into a pool, Jesus' idea that union between man and woman was sacred, a holy work of God, spread until it spiritualized marriage in every corner of the world. Today, even in Asia, churches are *the* place to get married. Christmas is a romantic holiday. Only Muslim countries still allow men to join with more than one woman, and Arab students tell me even in Saudi Arabia monogamy is fashionable.

****

"Give to Caesar what belongs to Caesar, and to God what belongs to God," Jesus said, in answer to another trick question.[16] This was practically Jesus' only word on politics. But from it, like an acorn growing into an oak, grew a concept under which much of the world now shelters: separation of church and state. In addition, modern democracy owes more than most realize to Jesus' words "My kingdom is not of this world."[17]

Finally, the Jewish carpenter also straightened twisted concepts of family loyalty by his simple words to Joseph and Mary in the temple.

Twenty years later he showed what "My father's business" meant when he picked up a whip and chased crooked businessmen out of the same temple. His disciple Paul was almost killed in a riot when he freed a slave girl from a degrading form of exploitation. Later disciples put an end to forced prostitution in countries from England to Japan. I know Christians who risk their lives today to fight the sex slave trade in Snake Alley, Hong Kong's Walled City, Thailand, and the Philippines.

A son can do other than die. A daughter is not a commodity. Their bodies, too, are Temples, set aside for the presence of God.

Jesus was history's most effective revolutionary and social reformer. Yet all the while, he walked the path of *Xiao*, showing the world a model of humility and proper loyalty like it had never seen before.

The Humility Of Jesus

Confucius leads us down a "Middle Path" to common-sense morality. Jesus takes us on a roller-coaster ride. The two men are going the same direction, but with Jesus, the *Tao* becomes an heroic adventure.

The journey begins with an earthward plunge.

Lao Tse wrote that he who was "without thought of self" would be able to "accomplish his private ends."[18] Chinese history is full of noble examples. Confucius passed up official posts to remain untainted. In the shadow of Qin's burial mound, Han Wen founded the great Han Dynasty by listening to people and avoiding pretense of god-hood. Nationalist founder Sun Yat-Sen won a revolution but in the interest of peace, allowed his rival to rule.

In the Gospels we find evidence that God had the same idea: that Absolute Power could accomplish great things in the guise of weakness.

The Christian doctrine of Incarnation, that in Jesus Heaven took on human flesh, is the perfect fulfillment of this ancient Chinese principle.

Even if we look at Jesus as just a human teacher, his humility is powerful. He knew what it was to use an elbow for a pillow. He was a "Friend of sinners": vagrants, lepers, prostitutes, quislings, and corrupt officials were drawn to him, and he became their friends. He gathered a handful of simple men, their hands wreaking of scales and fish guts, and told them, "Go change the world." And they did.

He told them: "You know that those who are looked at as rulers of the Gentiles lord it over them. . . But it must not be that way with you. Instead, whoever wants to take the lead among you must be everyone's servant. . . . For even the Son of Man did not come to be served, but to serve, and to give his life as a ransom for many."[19]

What Jesus Saw Within

The identity of Jesus is as controversial today as it was two thousand years ago. Who did he say he was? A revolutionary? Guru? Prophet?

The title "Son of God" bothers many. "Jesus would have been appalled to hear followers equate him with God," Some say. "It was John and Paul and the early Christian councils that invented the doctrine of the Incarnation."

Suppose you came around a bend in a jungle path and found yourself face-to-face with five hundred pounds of powerful, striped felinehood with claws. Would your situation or emotions be much different if you had never heard the word "tiger?" Would you blissfully continue on down the trail as if nothing had changed in your world? My guess is you would not.

If you enjoy such shocks, forget all dogmas and definitions, and read the Gospels on their own terms. The title "Son of God" is not what will change your world, it is the reality of whom you meet in them. If you blithely continue on your path afterwards, it is not your definitions, it is your eyes and ears that need to be checked.

Jesus spoke about himself in hints, metaphors, and stories. Many people say this is because he wanted to avoid trouble. Some liberal scholars say he wasn't really sure who he was.

But when I read a Gospel—just a page or two, in any place—such theories shatter like a vase at impact of a meteor.

The metaphors Jesus gave about himself light up the sky. Jesus called himself bread that brings eternal life.[20] Light that illumines the world.[21] The bridegroom of the church. A doctor who cures souls.[22] The "Son."[23] He was the one written about by the prophets.[24] He was "Lord" of the Jewish holy day.[25] He forgave sins.[26] He was "Greater than the temple," the home of God.[27] Compared to the Gospels,

Confucius' claim that "Heaven is the author of the virtue in me" was so modest it can hardly excite shock.

Jesus said *Tiger* in a thousand different ways, calmly painting a self-portrait that shatters our picture of the universe.

The word-pictures he used to describe himself wouldn't be so shocking, or the anger of the powerful so great, if they could explain him away as a madman. If Confucius, Mother Teresa or Winston Churchill said what Jesus said, we'd lock them up. What is frightening is, everything Jesus said and did fits naturally with this impossible self-image.

"The people were astonished at his teachings; for he taught them like a man with authority."[28] This astonishment shook the Jewish religious leaders to the bone. They weren't hostile towards authority as a concept—the attitude of our rebellious, smart-alecky, too-cool-to-be-fooled generation. No, authority was sacred to the Pharisees. But Jesus was a commoner, a carpenter's son. Yet his words were like a storm from a clear sky. It was not just threatening. It was unendurable.

Thus Jesus, like many Chinese, had the experience of being "struggled against," of being brought before a hostile crowd and beaten, insulted, and mocked. Even at his trial, it was the rulers of the nation who acted insecure. "Don't you know I can kill you?" One felt compelled to ask.[29]

Another hurled a final trick question at him. "Are you the Christ?" he asked.[30] His friends smiled; it was a clever move. "Yes" and they would have a right to stone him as a blasphemer. "No" would once-and-for-all put an end to his game.

Jesus spoke without riddles this time. "I am," he said. "And you will see the Son of Man coming in the clouds of heaven."

I think what Jesus' modern critics mean when they say Jesus was confused, is that like his ancient critics, they are confused by his lack of confusion. Jesus knew exactly who he was. As with Confucius, only much more so, it is the extent of Jesus' certainty that causes his critics to wonder.

Jesus, The Good Psychologist

The third form humility takes is an interest in other things and people. Not a single word of small talk has been preserved in all four Gospels. Nor did Jesus teach how to grow high-yield barley or build a faster chariot. Yet he noticed small things—seeds, birds, fish, coins—and used them to illustrate his lessons. The point of his stories was how a person can gain a right relation with God and his neighbors.

A scientist studies stars, wave dynamics, or the RNA of a tomato plant. Each can be a rewarding subject for years of research. But man is the most complex object we see.

One reason Jesus was credible when he talked about himself was the clarity with which he saw other people. He didn't set classes against each another. Nor did he claim that an end to patriarchy or imperialism or liberalism would heal the world's aches and wounds. Such are perennial tactics whereby simple rebels upset the shape of society, usually to allow oppression to reform in an even harsher shape.

Jesus dug deeper. He addressed himself to the rebel and manipulator within each of us. He set believers against the worst in themselves.

Many great thinkers—Tolstoy, Pascal, Dostoevsky—felt Jesus knew the heart of man better than anyone. One of America's most famous psychologists, Robert Coles, described his decades of labor as a "footnote" to the Sermon on the Mount.[31] Scott Peck implicitly called Jesus the "smartest man who ever lived."[32] When I read the Gospels, it's not hard to see why they say such things. But their praise, like the dogmas of the early church, seems oddly irrelevent. No one who reads the Gospels with himself as Judge and Jesus on trial, is really reading them. When we read his words, we are forced to see into our own hearts.

Father And Son

Jesus said that to be his followers, we must become "like little children." The first direction a child looks is up, at his parents.

Christianity is called a rival to Confucianism. But of all the religions and philosophies of mankind, only in "Jesus-teaching" do the Confucian ideals of *Xiao* and *Ren* attain transcendent significance. In the Bible, Confucius' teachings are both justified by the order of the universe and fulfilled in the climatic historical drama of the human race.

The Christian religion is a love story about a Father and a Son. In this story, the Father is the person who made the universe. Jesus is the son.

What is vague theory in the *Book of Poetry* and the *Analects* and in thousands of legends around the world becomes day-to-day reality in the Gospels. "Son of God" was not a fancy title to intimidate Jesus' followers, or a vague unity with the Ultimate: the "filial piety" of Jesus was something immediate, striking, and natural. He excused himself from teaching crowds and meeting officials to spend a day with *Shang Di*. His miracles drew attention, but, he said, "The Son can do nothing by himself; he only does what he sees his Father doing."[33] If death itself were a "cup" his Father offered, he would not refuse.[34] On the cross, the unaccustomed distance of his Father was a greater agony than the spikes in his wrists.[35]

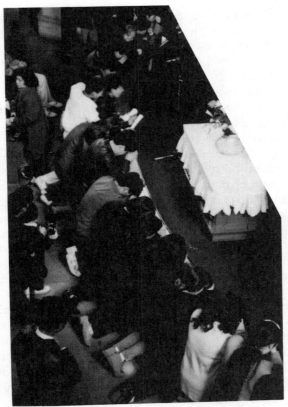

Reconciliation to Heaven, Shanghai.

Was this all a personal delusion? Jesus' unique power and authority argue that it was not. To all appearances, the relationship worked both ways. Jesus wielded power and authority like you would expect only from the True Son of Heaven. That also was something that scared Jesus' opponents.

If, following Jesus, we too can become "sons and daughters of God," consider how this would solve an ancient dilemna in Chinese morality.

Suppose you're a government official. The local police captain tells you one day, "Your son has been caught embezzling funds. I can get him off, though—as a favor to you." What do you do? Confucius' solution was to bend the rules for the sake of the son. It's easy to see his point. How can we put a family member in prison for an abstract principle?

Confucius' answer caused problems, though.

Even today social stability is threatened in China by corrupt officials who smooth the way for sons and daughters. Lazy students graduate to the best jobs; good ones are sent to backwaters for want of connections. If China explodes in the near future, nepotism will be the spark that ignites it, as it was in 1989.

Emperor Qin opted for rules over relationship. He made a real contribution to China by making public office a prize to be won through diligence rather than birth.

But Confucius had a point, too. The "rule of law" truly is something less than the rule of love.

For those who follow Jesus, this conflict disappears. We who have one Father are all brothers and sisters. From now on, our roles as parent and child, citizen and ruler, teacher and student, are not based on fear, bureacratic duty or patriarchal benevolence, but on the love of God that fills those who belong to Him.

There is room for rules. When human authority takes a step too far, though, we're free to rebel. China has seen in this century how Christians can stand up to priests and party chairmen and parents and say "NO!" "I have a Father in Heaven. I owe Him first allegiance."

This makes communist rulers nervous, by the way, especially when they remember what happened in Eastern Europe.

From the beginning Jesus' authority and subversive loyalty to God made the trigger-finger of rulers twitch.

It's one thing for a leader to call himself "lord" from a palace surrounded by walls and bodyguards. Even at the head of an army, or near a jungle where he can escape at the sign of trouble, big words can be spoken lightly. But suppose a rebel should march openly into the capital. Suppose his followers shout praises to God for the "new order" he brings. Suppose only a band of weak-kneed fishermen and a couple rusty swords stand between him and the Emperor. Imagine, to top it all off, he won't let his side fight.

What can you say about a revolutionary like that? Either he is a fool. Or he has a plan.

When Jesus entered Jerusalem for the last time, he came with a plan. George Orwell might have called it "doublethink." But Lao Tse or Confucius would have understood. His weakness was his strength. His death would accomplish the benevolence of Heaven.

The world was small, but the Father loved everyone in it. So the Son climbed his own Mount Tai, and painted East and West with his blood.

At this point the saga of the True Son of Heaven begins to touch on another paradox: one very near the heart of Chinese culture. It is the mystery of how sacrifice can be the prelude to joy.

Part III

Across The Silk Road

A company name in Seoul, Korea.

"Chun Lian" on a Shanghai door.
Top: "Gold and jade fill the hall."
Right: "Welcome spring meet Fu."
Left: "Congratulations, get rich."

On the wall of the
Confucian temple in
Confucius' hometown.

Vaudeville monkey act and portering goods up Mount Tai:
two unusual ways to make money in today's China.

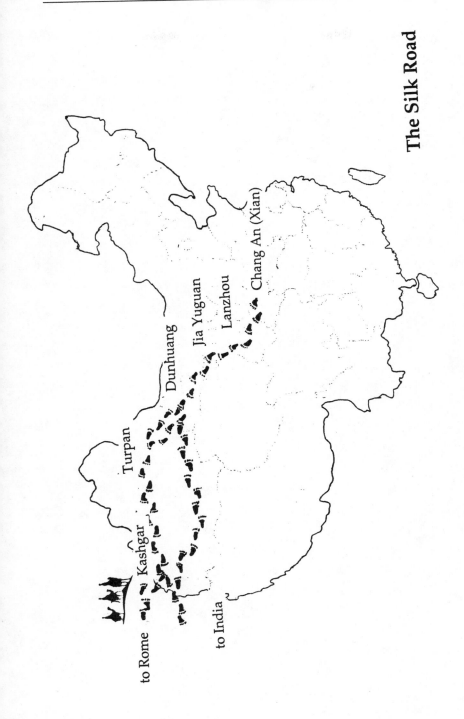

The Silk Road

Chapter Six

"Congratulations, Get Rich!"

Fu (福) may be the most popular character in the Chinese language. You see it upside-down over doorways. It names cities, mountains, rivers, restaurants, trucking companies, temples, even graveyards.

In Japan, where I type these words, 福 is pronounced *fuku*. The largest city on the island of Kiushu where I live is *"Fuku* Harbor." I look out the window and see *Fuku*-Land Parking Garage and *Fuku*-Sand-House Dutch cake factory. A "Big *Fuku*" is a sticky rice desert you buy in Chinatown with a strawberry or piece of banana in it. My wife's maiden name is *Fuku*-Island.

Often I notice 福 hanging in a garden or decorating a t-shirt in America, too.

Fu is composed of four radicals: God (衤), one (ˉ), mouth (口), and field (田). Thousands of years ago, the character consisted of "God" on the left, and the shape of a container used in sacrifice on the right. Eventually, the container evolved into these three other radicals.

By itself *Fu* means fortune, luck, happiness, and prosperity. "I have lots of *Fu*" means "I'm fortunate." "He gave them *Fu*," means "He blessed them." *Fu* can also be combined with *Xing*, *Qi* or *Fen* (興福 , 福气 , 福分) to mean "good fortune" or "happiness."

The fact that "God" was a part of happiness seems to have embarrassed the communists. When they came to power, they changed the left-hand radical to 衣, clothing. It's not hard to follow their logic. Even when a Chinese character evolves beyond recognizable shape of the original object, meaning still seems to cling to form more than with

65

A Kunming lady with something that hopped on two legs.

other languages. Besides, the theories of crackpot linguist Nicholas Marr that language is a product of class warfare, were at this time the rage in the communist world. The association between God and happiness was not one Mao could let stand.

The Chinese idea of happiness, like the shape of the character which represents it, may seem exotic to Westerners. But the idea touches on all the deepest human hopes, and even hint at the dangers that lie in our way as we pursue happiness. Real happiness does consist of drawing near to God. And satisfaction seldom comes without sacrifice.

As we look at these rich and enticing facets of Chinese culture, we'll see how some have been twisted into instruments of destruction. We'll consider how Buddha tried to reform *Fu* into a useful shape. We'll see why the foreign teaching failed to distract China from its desire for *Fu*, but that desire changed Buddhism instead. Finally, we'll see how Jesus brings happiness to China.

Noodles hanging to dry.

Have You Eaten Full?

Some of a visitor's most vivid memories of China are often formed at the dinner table. Chinese tables are round, so friends can laugh and shout and provoke each other from every direction. If the occasion is more formal, guests might be called on to sing a song or tell a story.

Chinese have asked me, "Do people in your country like food as much as us?"

Maybe so, but over thousands of years, Chinese chefs have created a cuisine of astonishing variety.

Some foreigners are afraid they'll be asked to eat stir-fried beagle, or saute of house cat, in China. If you wander into a certain restaurant in Shanghai, you really are given a choice of grasshopper, cicada, scorpion or ant. But it's an exclusive restaurant; no one dines there by accident.

Northern Chinese joke that in Guangdong (Canton) Province people eat everything with four legs but a table, everything with two legs but a man, and everything with wings but an airplane. At Cantonese wedding banquets, everything with scales, fins and a shell also appears on the table.

Meals in ordinary Chinese restaurants can be just as satisfying, and even more interesting. I ate in one *jiazi* restaurant so full of steam I had to hug the ground to see the next table. A Sichuanese restaurant used so much pepper I ran out on the street coughing a couple times before I even tasted the food.

Sitting in a seafood restaurant in Canton, I felt drops of water hit my arm. Where was it coming from? I checked the ceiling for leaky pipes. I watched waiters to see if they spilled tea on their way by. Still mystified, I moved to another table. Then a fat perch-like fish hurled out of a tank along the wall, bounced off the table where my food had been and landed on the floor.

Chinese like food fresh. In some restaurants you find not just fish, but cages of rustling chickens or pigeons, or sleepy weasels, snakes, deer or bats awaiting your order. For the faint-hearted, there are many tasty alternatives.

Eating at the home of Chinese friends may be the best of them. Nothing is more democratic or better for the appetite than with a group of friends hatching a batch of *jiaozi*, the succulent boiled dumplings northern Chinese love. Male, female, skilled and novice, (like myself) join in. After the meal, candy, watermelon seeds, and oranges appear on the table, with one of a thousand varieties of tea.

The most usual way to say "eat" in Chinese,吃饭, is to "eat rice." Rice is a symbol of Chinese civilization. Traditionally, the poor got by on yams or corn. "Hill people," and peasants during famine, ate wild weeds or even pine bark.

A symbol both of Mao's success and his failure is that under socialism, the poor learned to waste this precious grain. When I walked by student dorms in China, I learned to keep a watchful eye, for fear uneaten rice thrown through a window might catch me in the face. (Elderly ladies swept the grounds every morning.) The communists alleviated China's chronic food shortage, but unlike Japan and Taiwan, for many mainland Chinese people, socialism may have killed some of the traditional reverence and gratitude for the blessing of rice.

熱惱 *ReNao* "Hot And Noisy"

One of the best ways to enjoy China is to wander through a night market on a summer evening. Woks flare in the darkness. Noisy crowds throng tables, shouting *"Gan Bei!"* (Empty the glass!") Lanterns and cooking fires light your way to stalls where vendors sell noodles, barbecued pork, or chestnuts roasted in huge black woks.

Outside a new shop firecrackers explode not one at a time, but a six-foot cylinder, a fire-fight in a can. Plug your ears, step back, and focus your mind on the Western stereotype of the "Inscrutable" Chinese. Someone is celebrating. When he's done, you can resume coherent thought.

Few comments on a party, festival or city sound as gracious in Chinese as the word *renao*, "hot and noisy."

The colors red and gold say to the eyes what firecrackers say to the ears. "Celebrate good times!"

田 *Tian* **"Fields"**

My grandmother used to tell me, "I had a dream of you walking through a rice patty. Did you ever do that in China?"

As often as possible. Rice patties are fascinating places. Farmers till the sod behind patient behemoths, the water buffaloes. Later, women bend over to plant little seedlings a few inches apart. As they grow, they join in level, uniform fields, bright as well-kept lawns. By harvest time, the full grain waves in the breeze over an army of mud snails. White egrets fly in to pick them off one by one. In southern mountains, terraces rise one above the other for thousands of feet, forming patterns of unforgettable loveliness.

Near the Vietnam border.

A field near Guilin: beauty, promise...and hard work.

Peasants in China appreciate the beauty of a full field of grain in a different way. Most still remember what it felt like when the rice didn't grow.

The character *tian* (田) looks like a rice patty on level ground, with raised tufts of grass around the edges dividing it in four.

Why does the character福 contain a small 田? Historically-speaking, its presence is an accident. But level rice land is certainly basic to the Chinese idea of happiness. Unfortunately, the process of leveling it has on occasion caused grief to the environment.

馬
馬
虎
虎

"Horse and Tiger"

When I lived in Taipei, Taiwan, I often fled the concrete heat of the city on a bus to the mountains. An hour away a hundred foot waterfall thundered into a narrow canyon. At the bottom of this canyon flowed a wider stream, which reflected its tropical-green walls. Cool water flowed around huge boulders into several tantalizing pools. I often came to swim or just breath the fresh air.

One hot summer day, after I'd swum and explored the rocks, a young man from a nearby village came to dip in the same pool. We sat in the cooler water of the stream flowing from the base of the waterfall and chatted. The waterfall roared at our backs, with emerald mountains rising on all sides.

"Look!" cried my companion. A shiny-blue river bird was flying across the creek. I smiled, feeling in harmony with nature.

He picked up a rock and threw it at the bird.

This reaction was unfortunately not a fluke. Most wildlife in Taiwan, except for the remotest mountains, has been hunted to the vanishing point. Endangered Taiwan bears and deer peer at you from cages on busy Taipei streets. In mainland China, foxes, weasels, and all kinds of wild animals take their places on dinner menus. Men in mountain areas carry long, thin guns in hopes a bird crosses their path. Tibetans hawk bear claws and deer antlers on the streets of major cities, largely to overseas Chinese. The government of India has complained to China about hunters crossing the border after endangered species.

"*Mamahuhu*" Chinese say, "Not so good, not so bad" but literally "horse horse tiger tiger." Horse, as servant of man, represents good. Tigers, meanwhile, were declared a pest in the 1950s and almost exterminated from Siberia to the Himalayas. Chinese demand for tiger medicine has brought the magnificent animal to the brink of extinction, even in India.

Not that they'd have much room to roam in today's China. Deforestation along the southern border, once a storehouse of tropical plants and animals, is heartbreaking. The Dai minority describes those mountains as "Bare as a monkey's butt." On the Vietnam border, there is a clean break between cultivated crops and bare soil to the north and jungle to the south. Until streams stopped flowing in dry season and crystal-clear creeks turned muddy with unprotected top soil in the rainy season, the contrast seems to have been almost a point of pride to many Chinese. We are civilized, developed, "cultivated." They still live in the woods. It was a pity to watch fertile soil and uncut timber go to waste.

No nation has progressed from field to factory without some damage to the environment. Also, the communists romanticized big

Long life, too,
takes hard work.

Displays of
C h i n e s e
medicine on
a sidewalk.

industry and made development a point of national pride. But Chinese culture didn't hold them back much. In China you seldom come across anyone who fully grasps the problem, even among those who breath choked air and fish foul rivers.

Two otherwise admirable facets of *Fu* give even more urgency to this need, and create problems of their own:

長
壽

Chang Shou "Long Life"

When Westerners think of medicine, they usually picture a handful of pills, or a liquid in a little bottle. Chinese medicine often comes in a less-processed state: a fine powder, an antler, or a bag of mushrooms.

Serving at a Chinese church consisting mostly of older people, I came to the conclusion medicine is China's favorite amateur sport. I heard worshipers pass around private medical breakthroughs after the service like brownie recipes: "Try some Yunnan *Bai Yao* for that—it really worked for my asthma." Mt. Tai wood fungus is said to cure high blood pressure, arthritis or coughing. Popular prescriptions I didn't hear in church include tiger penis or snake blood to cure impotence.

Only a fraction of traditional Chinese cures have been tested in Western laboratories. How many valuable secrets are hidden on back shelves and in the knapsacks of herb salesmen? Health is an esoteric art in China, and many remarkable drugs are likely to vanish if folk medicine is neglected.

But China has also been cursed with its share of quacks.

A Taoist doctor in the late Ming dynasty cooked up a drug called the "Hung pill." First he added a compote of smoked plums to the menstrual discharge of teenage girls. Then he dried the mixture seven times, added milk, cinnabar, pine resin, and dried and powdered human waste. This he guaranteed would cure five kinds of fatigue, seven kinds of wound, and general disability.[1]

After they killed the Emperor Tai Ch'ang, Hung pills lost favor somewhat.

But doctors of like caliber have come out of the woodwork in recent years. Advertisements for Gonorrhea, syphilis, and AIDS "cures" replace the thoughts of Mao on many brick walls. Salesmen spread wares from field, forest and sea—including endangered species—on flannel tarps on sidewalks.

Meanwhile, the modern Chinese government markets "Long Life" cigarettes.

I traveled with a Chinese man whose good friend had just died of lung cancer at the age of thirty. Like a majority of Chinese men, he lit up whenever he could, admitting sheepishly, "I can't quit." Under Smoker-In-Chief Deng Xiao Ping, whose own long life is remarkable, a billboard at the Hong Kong border that once bore a portrait of Chairman Mao now shows the Marlboro Man.

Worse things than lung cancer are packaged in the name of long life. In a raid on a grimy seaside district north of Taipei, police arrested men, none under sixty, in the company of girls as young as eleven. The girls, of course, weren't volunteers.

Christians don't deny human life is precious. Stoics and plastic heros may sneer, but no one should be ashamed of fearing death. Nor does the fact that some pursue long life in the wrong way detract from its value. If a hundred thieves try to steal the same painting, doesn't that show it's worth something? Jesus said a human life is worth more than many sparrows. It is only proper and reasonable to hate death.

But unless the desire for *Chang Shou*, long life, is tempered and channeled, it ruins both those who feel it, and those who get in their way.

 Jin "Gold"

Few nations are as openly passionate about money as China.

You notice it all over. At Confucius' grave, a girl hawks books on Mao wearing a t-shirt which says: "Having money is just better than not having money." A twenty-three year old farmer carries tourists up Mount Tai for ten dollars a customer, more or less, depending on weight. In a small town, a party official plants orchids on his balcony to sell in the city. Near the border of Vietnam, a gold smuggler branches out into pornography, explaining that his models are American millionaires. At the Burma border, solid citizens smuggle Hyundai jeeps or jade, while quiet sorts in sun glasses bring heroin.

A survey of a few countries in Europe, North America, and Asia, revealed that people in Hong Kong and Taiwan put the highest value on wealth. I took my own survey which included mainland China asking the question, "What do you feel is the purpose of life?" Two young peasants gave me this simple answer: "To make money."

Making money seems an almost universal obsession in China. News shows take viewers on endless factory tours, always asking, "How did you strike it rich?" Perhaps the powers-that-be hope to get peoples' minds off politics. But, of course, Marxism also affirms man is an economic creature.

I'd be less sympathetic if I hadn't visited rural China, where many of the hungriest young entrepreneurs were born. In one village, I jotted down these notes:

"The house we went into was large. . . but was made of mud. There were a lot of holes in the wall."

74

"While we were talking some chickens walked in the front door. The young teacher whose house it was chased them out. He was embarrassed. I heard a lot of disclaimers like 'We're really backward' and 'This house isn't very good.' What could I say? I commented that in a lot of ways it's nicer to live in the countryside: it's more peaceful, for example. They didn't buy that."

In a larger town:

"Mr. Liang offered me hot water instead of tea. He was in the process of bringing home the most decrepid head of lettuce-like vegetation I have ever seen used, riddled and half-eaten by previous occupants, flimsy and sour-looking. He offered to lend me his bicycle, spending about ten minutes pumping up the tires of the rusty vehicle, which made me fell quite guilty."

In the same province, I watched a woman pull the plow for her husband. The family was, it seems, too poor for a water buffalo.

"Recruit wealth to enter."

This is the cauldron of poverty from which the new generation of Chinese capitalists is emerging. Kao Chin Yen, Vice Chairman of Taiwan's President Enterprise, a company that modestly plans to become the world's largest food company within a few years, (it only needs to grow 30 times) called losing money a "crime against society." If his company collapsed, he told an interviewer, he'd "feel like committing suicide." The poorest villages of China are good recruiting ground for men of similar temperament, he noted,

> "The people who achieve the most in business come from poor backgrounds. They struggle and are willing to take any challenge."[2]

The desire for financial security has been stifled for generations in China by war, revolution, and ideology. Now it has become a flood. Those who have never known hunger have little right to criticize. In its own way, what is happening in China today is a beautiful thing.

Gold is the ultimate expression of financial security. Gold lasts. It never rusts or loses its value.

The Chinese words for most metals—iron, lead, copper—and many other words—money, needle, spade, to engrave—are based on the gold radical. Taoist alchemists once ate gold and mercury in hopes of living forever. Even today, gold is sprinkled in some exotic dishes. Mercury, fortunately, is no longer favored as a cooking ingredient. Perhaps that is how the Chinese came to associate red and gold with royalty and celebration.

囍 *Xi* "Marriage Happiness"

"To be happy at home is the end of all human endeavor," wrote Samuel Johnson. If you treat your elderly relations with reverence and the young with kindness, taught Mencius, "The world may be made to go around in your palm."[3]

Some Chinese philosophers (men) maintained the ideal number of women for a man of means was four. You wouldn't want just one cup for a tea set, would you? They asked.

It's hard to think of anything that prevented happiness at home more than such self-serving theories. Yet practically the only man who said anything against it apart from the influence of Western ideas was Ku Yen Wu.[4] He left wife and home with a pile of books to preach celibacy. Now, Marxism is fading, wild facts about the personal life of Mao Tse Tung have emerged, and more and more wealthy men are taking extra "little wives."

Chinese history may not support the idea of monogamy, but the Chinese language does. The word *Xi*, "marital happiness," which you

Common sentiments. (On a t-shirt in Beijing.)

often see over doorways and on windows, is one example. In it two "joy" radicals—not five—depict wedded bliss.

China needs a true "Middle Way"—a theory of family that will fulfill, not undermine, Chinese culture, by finding a reasonable balance between extremes.

子 Zi "Child"

A foreigner who was sensitive to China's environmental problems visited a Chinese kindergarten. He went home philosophizing:

"That kindergarten is a wonderful place. It is safe, warm, bright, airy, clean and lovely. At six, those children will graduate to cold rooms, dangerous wiring, no plumbing, dirt, drabness and discomfort. . . . China's work is to make the whole country into that kindergarten."[5]

Offspring were security to Chinese peasants. The Chinese feeling for children is reflected in the language: the word for good, 好 (*hao*) is a picture of a mother and a child. In 1979, with over a billion Chinese, the government established a one-child per family policy which said, in effect, "Good enough already." The resulting shortage of children, especially in the cities where enforcement is strict, has caused people to cherish or even spoil them more than ever.

What Is *Fu*?

The Chinese aren't the only people who want safety, good food, money, long life, or children, of course. The pattern which these desires form in China is, however, as unique as the Chinese writing system. As in all cultures, there is danger in every ideal: danger of betrayal, of selfish indulgence, of grasping for a lesser good when a greater is offered. Modern China's polluted rivers and corrupt political system are a warning. But in its essence the Chinese love of life is natural, human, and honest. It's part of what makes China so intriguing: different, yet familiar.

Fu is a lock on the Chinese culture.

It closes the door to religions so spiritual they rob joy from life. We don't need to be ashamed of our animal desires; the mouth was formed to be filled with food, as the dirt was to grow plants. Yet it also implies God must be the foundation of our most basic pleasure. Man does not live by rice alone. We are also made to know God.

How do we attain ultimate happiness?

Nothing comes easy in life. Rice doesn't grow except by stomping through mud and bending over a thousand times. Marriage takes dowry and work. Pain comes before birth.

The Silk Road, the bloodline of commerce that once joined China to the West across Central Asia, is a symbol of this great truth. Chinese might prefer to call it the Gold Road: silk went west, and gold came east. But the way in either direction lay across some of the harshest deserts on the surface of the planet. To gain wealth, businessmen threw their cash away on what was basically a death trap. For a comfortable living, they gave up good food, or even life itself.

The Silk Road is a symbol of the sacrifice that true happiness demands of those who seek it. It is also the road over which both Buddhism and Christianity came to China. In order to fully appreciate how Jesus fulfills China's hopes for *Fu*, it is helpful to first consider Buddha and the role he played in China. It is a role he is beginning to play in the West, too.

Dai language researcher with Buddhist monks, Gengma, Yunnan.

Chapter Seven

Buddha Walks The Silk Road

Around 560 B.C., a baby boy was born in northern India. Confucius, who was born a few years later, would spend most of his life seeking political power. Siddhartha Gautama was born son of a king.

Gautama drank in with his mother's milk most of what China meant by *Fu*. His elephants were clad in silver. Silk and gold and rich meals were as natural an environment to him as bark is to a beetle. Attendants shielded the young prince from the gloomy side of life. At the age of sixteen he wedded a beauty named Yasodhara. Finally came a stroke of fortune that seemed to prove the blessing of Heaven was on him: his wife bore him a healthy son.

Yet Gautama felt oddly restless and dissatisfied. One day he took an outing from the palace and met a sick man, an old man, a corpse, and a monk.

The movie *Little Buddha* retells the story well. "Sick? What is that?" He asked his servant in puzzlement. "No one reaches the moment of death without falling sick at least once," the servant answered. "Even kings?" He asked. "And death—what is that?"

Deeply shaken by the answer, Siddhartha took a last look at his sleeping wife and son one evening, and stole out of his palace. His quest for an answer to the riddle of suffering would take six years.

Enlightenment came while Gautama sat under a Bhodi tree. Legend has it he sat rooted to the spot for forty-nine days, engulfed in the experience. When he came to, he was Buddha, the "Awakened One."

Buddha became aware of what are called the "Four Noble Truths." First, he saw that life meant suffering.

Second, suffering was caused by desire—not just lust for someone else's wife or a passion to blow up buildings—but ordinary hunger, thirst, sex drive, and other expressions of individual consciousness were the causes of human misery.

The really awful aspect of this suffering, to Buddha, was that it repeated over millions of life cycles. Many Westerners think of reincarnation as a romantic if unlikely hope. At one point in *Little Buddha*, a Tibetan monk talked to a Seattle yuppie about rebirth, and the American's reaction was, "I don't know if I believe in it but I'd like to."

Buddha didn't *want* to believe in rebirth. In the same movie, he called it a "curse." And of course, Buddha was right. Life has meaning as a story. But what if after every chapter, you forget the chapter you just finished? What if (to use another *Little Buddha* example) you make one false move and spend 500 lives as a goat? If the Asian view of reincarnation is correct, this world is like a slope in hell up which we each push our boulder, each time to have it crash down on us again.

To relieve this endless suffering—this was Buddha's third discovery —we need to rid ourselves of desire. Our hearts must become empty: *maya* in Sanskrit, *kong* in Chinese. It is only by training ourselves in disattachment that we can escape the trap of misery our egos set for us.

Buddha's final discovery was a methodology for breaking these bonds: right knowledge, aspiration, speech, behavior, livelihood, effort, mindfulness and absorption. This he called the "Eight-Fold Path."

For the next forty-five years, Buddha traveled India, setting people on the path he found to spiritual freedom.

Six hundred years passed before the first Buddhist missionaries made their way across the Himalayas. By now the movement had split into two. One group, the "Way of the Elders," *Theravada* Buddhism, emphasized the solitary search for enlightenment. But others asked, "Why, once Buddha was awakened, did he remain in the 'sea of sorrows' that is this world? Why not vanish at once into Nirvana?" *Mahayana*, "Big Raft" Buddhism, emphasized the compassion of Buddha and the need for believers to find the way together. Thus a seed of something like love was sown into what had been a rather stoic philosophy.

The "Way of the Elders" spread east, into tropical lowlands from Burma to the South China Sea. Hemmed on the north by malarial valleys and head-hunter-haunted spurs of the Himalayas, Theravada had little impact on China.

But the "Big Raft" was pushed by the current of destiny around the western edge of the mountains, onto the Silk Road. As a thistle attaches itself to an animal's fur and drops on ripe soil, so the seed Big Raft Buddhism brought with it would fix its roots deep in Chinese soil.

Journey To The East

Some say the star-gazers who visited Jesus at his birth may have come from China. If so, they could have run into the first group of Buddhist missionaries coming the other way.

The ideal of compassion had begun to develop a life of its own in Mahayana Buddhism. The term *Bodhisattva* had come into vogue. A Bodhisattva was a being who had been awakened as Gautama had, and like him, chose to remain in the world to save all living beings. An Indian work called the *Lotus* spoke of a god of mercy named

Mahayana Buddhism: All board the big raft.
(He River at Wen Zhou, Zhejiang Province.)

Avalokivara, "From on high looking down." "Guan Yin," he would be called in China.

As they passed through the harsh Central Asian desert, it may have crossed the monks' minds that they, too, were like Guan Yin. They risked bandits, wild animals, mountain storms, and the desert for the salvation of their hosts. They'd have to learn a new and difficult language. Who knows how they'd be received? Buddha himself only promised that "Some will listen."

Did China listen to the message the monks brought? The obvious answer, reached by a superficial glance at China's temples and even the artwork in the caves along the Silk Road, is it struck paydirt. Chinese converted to Buddhism. But take a close look at what China calls "Buddhism." Then you see all that stuck in Chinese soil was one seed. And when it grew and spread its branches, it took more the form of a Palestinian cross than an Indian Bhodi tree.

What Is "Chinese Buddhism?"

Around Dragon Mountain in Taipei spreads a bustling and *renao* night market district. Papaya, pineapple, mango and guava are piled high on carts. Illegal hawkers pick up and run when they hear the police coming. Licensed stalls sell oyster omelet on a leaf of Chinese cabbage, smothered in thick, sweet brown sauce. Turtles, octopus, deer and dogs wait in cages for diners. In other stalls, acrobatic monkeys and scantily-dressed singers and weight-lifters show off for the crowds.

Foreigners call the market Snake Alley. Three or four shops sell snake blood. The snakes are kept in cages, each new sacrifice hanging from a hook in front so its blood drains into a glass. In three dark lanes at one end of Snake Alley, teenage girls wait behind the bars of their own pink cages. Snake blood is supposed to increase a man's sexual potency.

Dragon Mountain Temple blends into these surroundings like a lily in a pond. As you walk through the gate, old men offer to tell your fortune. Young men sell pornographic videos. Women hawk lotus petals. Heavy-set monks sell blessings. A crackle of fireworks fills the sky and a cloud of acrid smoke blurs the yellow *M* of the McDonalds across the street. In the courtyard, men gather to talk about Taiwan independence. Another day, a stage has been set up for Chinese opera. Whatever the action, stone dragons on the roof "look down from on high" in tolerant good will.

Every day thousands of Chinese make their way under those dragons, past billowing clouds of incense, to the inner courtyard. They bow before idols, the "host" goddess in the center, "guest" deities set up in a row along the back wall. Each idol is surrounded by a kitchen-cabinet of colorful retainers.

Dragon Mountain is Taipei's oldest "Buddhist" temple. It was completed twenty-six years before the founding of the United States. Here, under carved scenes from the *Romance of the Three Kingdoms*, Chinese have come to worship, talk politics, ask gods to settle lawsuits, or people-watch, for almost three centuries.

Most of the people in the streets outside will tell you they're Buddhists. Within, women sit in front of an Indian deity, finger rosary beads, and mutter a chant Gautama might have understood, but most of them do not: "*A mi tofo, a mi tofo.*"

Temples like Dragon Mountain have been an important part of Chinese religious life for hundreds of years. Purer sects gather huge crowds, such as the fifty thousand who came to hear "tele-evangelist" Xing Yun on one occasion. Buddhist temples dot mainland China. After forty years of Marxist education, a hundred fifty million Chinese still say they're Buddhist. Nevertheless, little or nothing that goes on around this temple or practically anywhere in China has much to do with the teachings of Gautama.

At the Institute For Buddhism Studies in Beijing, a researcher told me:

> "Buddhism doesn't really fit China—Indian Buddhism. But Chinese Buddhism changed so it fits Chinese. Thinkers, writers, artists, all were greatly influenced by Buddhism. But they didn't believe in Buddhism. How did they show they didn't believe? They wanted to get married, work as government officials. . . Buddhism encourages people to become monks. We Chinese really place a high importance on marriage."

Taiwan Chinese have more temples per capita than anyone else in the world. Most Taiwanese answered my survey by telling me they went to the temples and believed in Buddhism. They had positive feelings towards Siddhartha: "With great compassion he saves people who are in distress." "(He was) a person who loved people." But, when asked the purpose of life, few if any said "to escape suffering" or "to attain detachment." Almost no one believed in reincarnation. The only one of the Four Noble truths that seemed to have stuck in most minds was the idea of right conduct, thought and attitude, which in any case Chinese believed long before Buddhism came to China.

If I were to pick an antonym for what the vast majority of Chinese really think, it might be "Buddhism."

"Buddhism With Chinese Characteristics"

It is said when fish first ventured onto land, they developed lungs and legs to help them survive. Buddhism was a fish out of water in China. At Dragon Mountain Temple you can see one way Buddhism evolved to cope with the new environment: Pure Land Buddhism. Guan Yin, the sprout that sprung from the Lotus seed from India, is the chief deity of that temple, and a good sample of the Pure Land sect. We'll look closer at Guan Yin in the next chapter.

Another direction Buddhism evolved was Zen. Zen, which has been compared to the Jesuit movement, on one level recaptured the spirit of early Buddhism with its strict discipline. In a sense it went beyond Gautama's teachings. In Zen, not only desire, but the whole material universe, was a trap for the senses:

> "The Outward-Appearance of things is not other than Emptiness; Emptiness is not other than the Outward-Appearance of things; their Outward Appearance is, in other words, this very Emptiness; Emptiness is, in other words, this very Outward Appearance. Sense is also Emptiness. . . Every particle of everything is Empty."[1]

The emptiness of all things was best discovered not through prose but through riddles. What is the sound of one hand clapping? Can you make a mirror with bricks?

The only answer was silence. . . until the moment when, either by meditating on a *gongan* as such riddles are called, or by some other discipline, the world suddenly transformed itself before your eyes. You saw through the material illusion. Often the moment of release brought laughter and an exhilarating sense of freedom.

Not many walked the long route of meditation and often seemingly bizarre ritual to Zen enlightenment. But the conclusion those who did came to, while shocking to those who had yet to see, was often reassuring in a typically Chinese way. The truly enlightened person may be he who, having seen that the "outer appearance" of things is illusory, henceforth lives a fairly normal life.

A modern Chinese philosopher, Fung Yu-Lan, explained:

> "The most important development in Chinese Buddhism was its attempt to depreciate the other-worldliness of original Buddhism. This attempt came close to success when the Ch'an (Zen) Masters stated that 'in carrying water and chopping firewood, therein lies the wonderful Tao.'"[2]

He noted, though, that even Zen masters stopped short of equating the *Tao* with raising a family or serving in government. If they had relaxed so far as that, their teaching would have "ceased to be Buddhism" at all. And most Zen teachers did not want to cut their slender remaining links to the historical Buddha.

Perhaps that's why Zen never won the hearts of most Chinese.

Zen did color the Middle Kingdom's imagination. It brought China an authentic "cultural revolution," not like Mao by burning and erasing the old, but by inspiring artists with new visions and images of peace, paradox and discovery.

But Zen did not prompt a religious revolution. A few among the intellectual elite plunged into the wave of enlightenment. But most merely dipped their toes in the surf. China's peasants, meanwhile, never went near the beach.

The Wisdom And Folly Of Buddha

There is much in Buddhism that could have "given *Fu*," been a blessing, to China.

Two treasures from the Buddha's bag are precious as gold in modern China: emptiness, and silence. Say this ten times to a Hong Kong bank manager, "Gold is not other than empty." The morning after a Cantonese wedding banquet, hear your stomach growl, "ascetisism is path to peace."

After a few days of walking through Canton's sultry grey streets, or standing on Shanghai's crowded buses as they nose through the exhaust, a weariness sets in. When mountains for miles around are denuded of all but runt pines, when jack-hammers sing soul-less tunes and black exhaust wafts across the street like fog from a pond of sorcerers, the ancient firs and cedars in Buddhist compounds soothe the mind. You feel as Gautama must have felt, trapped in his castle, the sky or a distant gleam of snow off the Himalayas giving his soul a breath of refreshment.

Buddhism has impressed the world with its ideals. Even the West may have been touched deeper than it knows. "Compassion," "Tolerance," "Unselfishness," and "Pacifism" rank high on the list of virtues Americans admire. No wonder: the West is in an introspective mood, and more eager to refrain from doing harm than to do good—a frame of mind suited to the Buddha's teachings and example.

But those teachings weren't the antidote China needed to materialism. Buddha was too one-sided. He showed half the truth, and not the half that counted most.

Consider Buddha's great act of renunciation, for example.

A famous American psychologist, Scott Peck, once counseled a man who was at a crossroads in life. Two choices before him were Zen Buddhism and a New Age commune. The third choice was to look up his three children, whom he hadn't seen for years.

Dr. Peck, who learned a lot about paradox through studying Zen, often writes of his admiration for Buddha. Yet when it appeared this patient had opted to dump his kids and launch out again on his spiritual quest, Dr. Peck groaned at his choice. Why? If running out on your family is admirable in the 6th Century B.C., why criticize it in the 20th Century?

One Buddhist pictures how Gautama:

"Gave the dear children of his own breast to be brahman's slaves. . . when he saw them flogged. . . he did not interfere. . . when the children were lamenting and said to him, 'Father, this ogre (i.e., evil spirit) is leading us off to eat us,' he did not comfort them."[3]

The Buddha myth lends itself to sadism. Buddha called his boy "Obstacle." No matter how often later apologists talk of Buddha's compassion and desire to save all sentient beings, I doubt the historical Siddhartha's noble act made a good impression on his in-laws.

A modern Buddhist named Qing Hai ("Emerald Sea") followed Gautama's lead. Born in Vietnam, she married an "extremely compassionate" German doctor. But "Even such a perfect and loving husband the Master still forsook because of the desire to help all sentient beings."

"Every day she prayed that if there were others who wanted to leave home, let them have all favorable conditions, never having to learn such pain that both she and her husband had for (the holy) cause!"[4]

"For the sake of all beings," she "put down every sentimental consideration" and slipped out of town.

Qing Hai's followers even praise her "great renunciation." Break a commandment, break a heart, and you're a saint. What a life.

Most Chinese admired Buddha like Peck admired him, in the context of the Buddha-myth, without looking at the faces of the people who had to foot the bill.

Leaving his wife was only one facet of Gautama's error. It seems to me people are even more liable to this blunder today than in 600 B.C. — perhaps because technology has expanded the ranks of those who have never known real hunger or poverty. Our crime, like his, is to take the good things in life for granted.

Is Life Only Suffering?

Snowflakes melt in the palm of your hand. Each is as brilliant as a diamond. An insect flits between blades of grass, like a tiny cruise missile.

My baby stares into my face and smiles. With his "hundred faces" as the Japanese say, he explores our apartment.

I know he'll suffer as he grows older. The world is a harsh place. But it's also a beautiful place, full of marvels and thrills. I cannot and will not teach him to be "detached" from desire. I pray only he learns when to grasp and when to let go, and where to seek that most worth holding.

Buddhism may be attractive to many in the West because like Gautama, most have more than they need. Paradoxically, self-control and a dash of asceticism may be the way to recovering child-like wonder. This may be why Zen, while telling us "every particle of everything is empty," created an art that brings to fullness the beauty in a carp or a branch of cherry blossoms.

Buddha saw that we travel through a desert. But he didn't see what was on the far side of it. He didn't understand that desire should lead us into and through that desert to a better place.

In one scene of the movie *Little Buddha*, a monk explained reincarnation by breaking a cup of tea. The tea ran over a desk and disappeared in the cracks of the floor. "The vessel breaks at death, but what it contains merely changes form," he seemed to imply.

But to Christians, as to traditional Chinese, man isn't the tea. He's the mug. We are not that which fills, but that which waits—heart, body, soul, mind—to be filled.

To kill desire for spiritual fellowship with beings who are external to ourselves and different is to kill our humanity. It is indeed like giving our children over to an ogre. Yet in another scene this same monk showed how even trained Buddhists have too much of the image of God on their souls to fully give their hearts to the ogre called "detachment."

The Old Master died and was buried, his successor found. The American boy was ready to go home. The Tibetan monk who brought him to India from America choked back tears as he said goodbye, saying to the boy's father, "I'm afraid I'm not a very good example of Buddhist detachment."

The viewer couldn't help but admire him for these words. What a remarkable admission! What a remarkable indictment of the Buddha's teaching! We simply cannot admire a person who in his relationships shows neither sadness nor joy. Even the actor who played Buddha was far from "detached" from his family or his friends. That's why he won our hearts.

To avoid suffering, a person may harden himself against feeling. But his heart is a garden of God's making, fertile and ready to sprout any wayward seed of His love. It's the theme of many movies. It's also the truth behind China's greatest myth.

Typhoon Sarah dropped up to 53 inches of rain in one day, tore this freighter out of Hualien Harbor and ripped her in two, killing two crew members. Before the days of weather satellites, such storms were the bane of fishermen. China prays for a Savior from life's storms.

Light in the darkness, or a siren-call to nothingness?
Dragon Mountain Temple, Taipei.

Chapter Eight

Guan Yin: "I Will Be There, When You Call. . . Symbolically

Once there was a woman in Guangdong Province who, when she passed middle age, gave her husband two concubines. After a time one captured his heart, and he neglected his wife. She died in regret, and her son grew up bitter against the younger woman.

One day the family took a picnic to a remote area, where, they heard, bandits were on the prowl. Finding himself alone with his step-mother, he decided to murder her, thinking blame could be pinned on the bandits. But the concubine realized what the son was up to, and cried out to the goddess *Guan Yin*. The son was unable to lift a finger against her. Later, having become an official in Taiwan, he told an American friend,

> "That woman was thoroughly immoral, a creature full of malice amounting to cruelty, the very opposite of the common run of Kuan Yin devotees. Yet she had triumphed over death for no other cause than absolute conviction of the compassionate Bodhisattva's desire to save every kind of sentient being whatsoever. Had Second Mother been a devil or a vampire fox it would have made no difference."[1]

Guan Yin's calm and compassionate face can be seen everywhere in East Asia. An aura surrounds her head (alone of all Chinese deities) and from her side a thousand arms reach out to save. Her white robes glow. Rough stone Guan Yins bless Japanese villages from the peaks of hills. Colorful cloth Guan Yins wait in temples across China to hear prayers of believers. In Taiwan, even the sea goddess *Matsu* comes second in popularity. To rescue those in danger, she appears as male or female, human, divine, animal, or even as a flower, it is said. She is very *"ling,"* say her worshipers. She has the "right stuff" in the spirit world.

E. T. C. Werner, in his book *Myths and Legends of China*, wrote of Guan Yin,

> "Other gods are feared, she is loved; others have black, scornful faces, her countenance is radiant as gold, and gentle as the moon beam; she draws near to the people and the people draw near to her."[2]

Who is Guan Yin?

In the last chapter I talked about the book *Lotus* which Buddhist monks brought with them from India. Actually only one chapter of that book, the seventeenth, talks about *Avalokitsvara*, or Guan Yin. But the pictures it painted were tantalizing:

> "Were you pursued by evil men
> And crushed against the Iron Mountain,
> One thought of (his) saving power
> And not a hair would come to harm."[3]

Buddhist scholar C. N. Tay summed up the remarkable promises of that chapter:

"(He) protects merchants bearing precious jewels from robbers, sailors from shipwreck, criminals from execution. By his help women obtain the children they desire. Fire ceases to burn, swords fall to pieces, enemies become kind-hearted, bonds are loosened, beasts flee, and snakes lose their poison."[4]

The fundamental teachings of Buddha fell on stony ground in China. But this one tiny seed sprouted into a fragrant vine which covered East Asia.

Why was China so ready to believe in Avalokitsvara? To find the answer, let us look first at the name, and then the myth, he clothed himself with on the far end of the Silk Road.

"Guan Yin"—What's In A Name?

When something new comes to China, the Chinese usually coin a local name, rather than borrowing a foreign appellation. Television, for example, became *"dian shi,"* "electric sight," in Chinese. The Japanese, by contrast, call it *"telebi."* When Coca-Cola came to China, the company called its beverage *Ke Kou Ke Le*—"tasty and delightful," or roughly, "May the mouth find happiness."

The Buddhist monks arrived among a people with dry spirits. The Chinese were as thirsty for *Fu* as the desert they had passed through was for water. The writer of the *Lotus* seemed to know what ordinary Chinese wanted: children, food, a cure for snakebite, protection against animals and bandits. Guan Yin was Buddhism packaged to sell in China; "Yunnan Bai Medicine" with a warm smile and a gentle touch. Medicine might cure the body. Here was something that went all the way to the soul: Salvation from Heaven with a human face.

The name *"Yin"*—sound—reflected the hope Guan Yin would hear. *Yin* also sounds like the *Yin* of *"Yin"* and *"Yang,"* the "mysterious female" Lao Zi spoke of. Perhaps this is why an Indian god became a goddess in China, and many women especially looked on her as their truest friend.

The Power Of Love In A Chinese Myth

In 1102, the Buddhist monk Pu-ming passed on a similar dream-picture about a local goddess named Miao Shan.

Miao Shan was a lovely princess of long ago, the youngest of three daughters of a king. She refused to marry her father's choice for a husband. Angered, the king locked her up in the Nunnery of the White Sparrow. But her continued good cheer won the favor of the gods. This made her father even madder, and he had his daughter murdered.

Her body was carried off by a tiger and preserved in a forest. Her spirit descended into hell, but hell went to the dogs in her presence. Irons fell off prisoners. Ogres learned to smile. In short, the underworld began to lose its deterrent value. So Miao Shan was exiled by the powers-that-be to the island of Puto, in Zhejiang Province. (Now a center of Guan Yin worship.) After nine years, she was deified.

The king became sick. Miao Shan came to him. Plucking her own eyes out, she cured him. Moved by her noble gesture, he repented, and she was made whole again.[5]

How did this native Chinese myth relate to the tales of the Indian god Avalokitvara? Miao Shan became a Chinese agent of the new religion, an "incarnation" of Guan Yin, as Guan Yin was of Buddha.

It's not hard to see the advantages of such a move. First, it provided a Chinese face for the new religion. Second, it played on the Chinese moral ideals of loyalty to parents and of self-sacrifice.

The ideas Buddha preached—life is suffering, desire is empty— did not appeal to most Chinese. Most of Buddha's moral teachings were admirable enough, but the example of a foreigner who ran away from home could hardly inspire a nation whose heros, like Miao Shan, were those who sacrificed all for their parents. Even Siddhartha's heroic renunciation of pomp and pleasure could add little to the reply Taoist philosopher Hsu Yu was said to make when offered half the world:

> "The tit, building its nest in the mighty forest, occupies but a single twig. The tapir, slaking its thirst from the river, drinks only enough to fill its belly. You return and be quiet. I have no need of the world."[6]

Confucianists replied to Hsu Yu and the Taoists as they would later reply to the Buddhists: "But does not the world have need of you?"

By putting forth the myth of Guan Yin, in all his/her guises, Buddhism tried to have it both ways. Escapism for the monkly-minded. Help for the masses. Buddha would renounce the world and save it at the same time.

"Yes, the world has need of me," Guan Yin said. "I will save it, even if I have to die. My love can overcome death."

Buddhism spread in China through myths of redemptive suffering, of the power of love to overcome hatred, and fancy footwork on the part of a few monks. But what spread was no longer really Buddhism. It was a dream: a dream of divine heroism that would save man regardless of cost to itself: of Jesus, in fact.

Do Buddhists Believe in Guan Yin?

Miao Shan and other stories about Guan Yin come in classic myth form. "Beautiful third daughter of cruel king attracts jealousy and admiration of immortals." The Greek tale of Cupid and Psyche begins exactly the same way. Psyche was even kicked out of hell for the same reason as Miao Shan.

The tales of Guan Yin in the great Buddhist allegory *Journey to the West* are a bit different, but not a whit more realistic or historical. That isn't a criticism. These are tall tales, meant to entertain and inspire.

Buddhists seldom ask whether these stories are true or not. According to C. N. Tay, the question "is of no concern to the author of the *Lotus*."[7]

Guan Yin is a symbol, said Tay. He quoted the Jewish scholar Yossi Dan:

"The symbol represents the unknown. Besides the symbol, we have nothing. Therefore, we must cherish it, and worship it."[8]

The idea that "fact" is less important than "truth," that a story can be wrong in historical detail yet embody deep revelations about life, seems eminently likely to many today.

John Blofeld claimed one night a Guan Yin idol spoke to him. Or did it? He was fuzzy on the details. But it was a pivotal moment for him. From then on, he wrote, he became her "devoted follower." Not that he "quite believed in her." In fact, his devotion had "nothing to do with belief." [9]

Blofeld's theory was Guan Yin corresponded to some kind of "energy" in his mind. The stories of Guan Yin themselves were "deliberate human creations," he admitted. On the other hand,

"The 'reality' of the Bodhisattva is not hard to accept, once one recognizes that even. . . Elephants and mountains are all creations of mind and therefore on a par with dreams, imaginings, visions. . . "

Blofeld felt philosophers and scientists were coming around to the idea that the universe is a "mental creation." One wonders if he imagines his reading public as also belonging to the Universal Mind, and if so, why he goes to so much work to communicate with it. Also, if scientists and philosophers are part of the illusion, what difference does it make what they think?

"An actual energy in the mind."

This is a good Zen explanation of Guan Yin. But is that what Chinese peasants prayed to?

The Tai Ping rebels and Communists understood that mental energies and symbols are no substitute for dry ammunition when a dragon has gone mad. When the emperor stormed or the Pearl River flooded after a typhoon, or famine ate away at the last of the grain, "dualism" between supplicant and Savior, far from "the most dangerous of errors," as Blofeld called it, was the only hope of the poor and oppressed.

Guan Yin: Shadow In Search Of A Tree

In Guang Xi province, a young man sat next to me on the bus. He was born, he told me, in the early 1960s. "My brothers are tall like you" he told me.

He was lucky to grow up at all.

In a rural county of the same province, I saw a book of annual population statistics. In three years of the late 1950s, the population grew from ninety thousand to one hundred thousand. The next three years, it *dropped* ten percent. In other words, twenty percent of the people disappeared.

Where did they go? A survivor told me, "We went up into the mountains and hunted for wild vegetables. We even ground tree bark down for flour. . . There was no rice, and we were very hungry."

Something had to go in the stomach. When there was no rice, they ate tree bark. Unfortunately it had little nourishment, and many died.

People are hungry for a kind face behind the Cosmos. When *Tian* becomes distant, legends like Miao Shan spring up. When statues of Buddha are smashed, posters of Mao Tse Tung go up.

Buddhism, by denying personality, left this fundamental human itch unscratched.

Yves Raguin wrote in *Areopagus* Magazine,

"We may say that Buddhism, which denied 'God' at the beginning, has been searching for a loving and living God. There is no other way to explain the development of the cult of the Buddhas in Mahayana Buddhism. These Buddhas. . . . are really personal manifestations of the Absolute."[10]

John Blofeld complained that the cross, with its blood and death, is an ugly symbol. This is one reason he looked to Guan Yin to fill his spiritual needs. But as the stomach is made for food, so the mind is made for truth. A starving soul can try to satisfy itself on substitutes. But a myth, however beautiful or admirable, cannot take the place of something real.

A myth is a shadow, a picture, a sketch of hope. It is not historical, and seldom pretends to be. Take it too seriously, as more than a story, and it becomes a cruel deception, like grass and tree bark to an empty stomach.

Buddhist monks invented and adopted the stories of Guan Yin to fill a felt need. Guan Yin was loved not only (like that other spiritual placebo, Santa Claus) for the gifts she brought. She was cherished as a hint that mercy might ultimately reign in the universe.

But China's revolutionary tradition reminds us that mercy must start with justice, at times even violent justice. In a fallen world, we need a God who takes sides. The cross is ugly because there are oppressors, and because God wants us to know He is on the side of their victims.

Why China Needs An Intolerant Savior

It was a raid. The police swooped with lightening speed on Taipei's most infamous criminal district, Snake Alley.

The police came on a mission of mercy. They came to free young victims of a vicious trade in flesh, who had been treated without a trace of human decency.

The snakes, that is. They were endangered species.

Brothel owners had little to worry about, even with a police station just a block away. For one thing, many of them were retired policemen. The rest, as one later told me, sent little red envelopes each month to friends in the station.

Nor did fear of the gods restrain them. The gods, too, seemed on the side of the oppressing classes. Mafia gangs in Taiwan form around Taoist temples.

Dragon Mountain Temple, the Buddhist place of worship on the same block as the police station, also got a cut. Guan Yin has been worshipped there for a hundred years without disturbing business. She reaches out her thousand arms to the brothels, one for each girl in that district, and draws back. . . cash.

Guan Yin, for all her theoretical compassion, didn't change much in China. She taught some people like the Taiwan official mercy. But she didn't feed the hungry or inoculate the sick. One ex-Buddhist wrote that no Chinese Buddhist has made a contribution to science. It was communism, borrowing technology from the West and zeal from missionaries, that put an end to foot-binding, gave women an education, and rescued girls from prostitution.

There's something in 'detachment' that could have balanced the Chinese zest for material riches. Why didn't it?

Chinese Buddhists strike a compromise with the material world.

For one thing, despite Buddha's talk of a "Middle Path," he went to an extreme. It was the opposite extreme from mainstream Chinese culture, but that only made it easier to ignore. If sexuality is part of the delusion that binds us, for example, why get especially upset about prostitution? All unions are "unclean." The common people, knowing in their hearts sex can be holy, realized Buddha was a little crazy and tuned him out—even when he talked sense.

Buddhists did talk sense about sex sometimes.* But calmly. There was too little passion in Buddha's compassion. He didn't nag, scold, harangue, threaten, bully, or clang gongs in pimps' ears.

Why should he? Buddhist love meant seeing "you" and "I" are one: vampire foxes and rabbits, thugs and junior high girls. And *karma* means everyone is getting what he or she deserves.

The world needs a Savior who loses his temper, who pounds tables and smashes hell to save an innocent child. We need a Savior who can curse as well as bless.

China knows this. It is why Mao built an army. It is why China cheered that army to victory. Mao also realized he needed to show China a face of transcendent love to keep her attention . Mao found his "Guan Yin" not in the nunnery of the White Sparrow, but in a monastery called the Red Army.

---

*Though monks often had a local reputation (unlike their other-worldly image in the West) for violence, greed and debauchery. The number one medical problem missionaries to Tibet encountered was sexually-transmitted diseases. Women were looked on as common property, and one missionary recalls a pretty 17-year-old girl known as 77, for the number of men who'd had her.

Guan Yin Joins The Army

Lei Feng was a young soldier who went above and beyond the call of duty. He cleaned clothes for his mates. He helped old people cross the street. He served in every way he could. Every night he wrote a diary, which was published after he died in a traffic accident.

"Learn from Lei Feng!" His fresh, ruggedly handsome face peers out from under a heavy northern winter coat in as many posters in mainland China as there are Guan Yin idols in Taiwan. The face and the slogan even appear on the computerized arrival and departure screen at the White Swan airport in Canton. What should Chinese learn from this semi-mythological citizen-warrior? Self-sacrifice. Compassion.

Taoism also evolved to accommodate China's desire for a Savior who would bring "help to the masses."

Early Taoist philosophers taught people to face death calmly. A disciple of Zhuang Zi found his master singing by his wife's grave. Zhuang Zi explained,

> "When she had just died, I could not help being affected. Soon, however, I examined the matter from the very beginning. At the very beginning, she was not living, having no form, nor even substance. But somehow or other there was then her substance, then her form, and then her life. Now by a further change she has died. . . for me to go about weeping and wailing would be to proclaim myself ignorant of the natural laws."[11]

The Taoism that captured the hearts of emperors who looked for "herbs of the immortals" on Mount Tai, and the Chinese masses, was less stoic. It appeared for no other reason than to overturn the law of death. According to Fu Yu Lan, the teachings of popular Taoism:

> "Are not only different: they are even contradictory. Taoism as a philosophy teaches the doctrine of following nature. . . The main teaching of the Taoist religion is the principle and technique of how to avoid death, which is expressly working against nature."[12]

Intellectuals like Dr. Fu scorn the hocus-pocus quackery of religious Taoists. But the error of the magicians was not in what they desired. It was in what they neglected in order to pursue it. In contrast to the most beautiful myths of Chinese tradition, and to the example of the Silk Road, they sought blessings for themselves by inflicting pain on other people.

Teachers like Zhuang Zi were wiser in many ways. But what price in humanity does a man pay to sing cheerfully at his wife's still-warm grave? Surely the quacks and sorcerers, and the common people of every rank they appealed to, were right to want, however vainly, to do something practical about death?

Chinese archeologist and historian Wang Kuo-Wei wrote,

> "I have been tired of philosophy for a considerable time. Among philosophical theories, it is a general rule that those that can be loved cannot be believed, and those that can be believed cannot be loved." [13]

Chinese philosophy and mythology cry for a Savior who can be believed *and* loved. China has been looking for One who comes to fulfill, not do away with, the ancient hunger for *Fu*. A Savior who is real. A living, historical person who will make the sacrifice that brings Heaven's love to Earth.

A tree takes root in China. (The author in a Buddhist village.)

Chapter Nine

Jesus On The Silk Road

Four unusual events occurred in the skies between May of 7 B.C. and July of 5 B.C. In the first six months of the 26-month period, three times the planets Jupiter and Saturn appeared to join. The fourth event, recorded only by Chinese astronomers, was the appearance of a nova, an exploding star, in Aquila Constellation, so bright it could be seen in the daytime.[1] About a year later, first-century tax collector Matthew says men "following a star" appeared in Jerusalem "from the east." They said the star was leading them to an infant "born king of the Jews."[2]

Where did they come from? Why did they want to see this child? What did they find?

Suppose they came over the Silk Road from China. Suppose one left a diary.

Diary Of A Han Astronomer

Han Year 199 November 22

Last night Lao Xing and I watched as the Wood star and the Earth Star met again. This hasn't occurred for hundreds of years, yet it was the second time this year. What does their conjunction mean for the court? I'll leave the official report to Lao Xing. But it peaked my curiosity, and I had a talk with my friend Da Cin Er, one of the refugees from the far West, whom the court has retained as advisor.

Da explained that among his people the Wood Star ("*Udi Idim*" he called it) signified their capital—which, like *Chang An*, is named

"Peace"—"Jeru's Peace." The Earth Star (*Mul Babbar*) signifies royalty. Furthermore, yesterday was a special festival celebrating the mercy of Heaven in their land—the *Day of Atonement,* he called it.

What could the stars be saying? It would be worth seeing what kingly mercies Heaven is preparing in this western city of peace.

Year 200 January 4

I've talked over the possibility of an expedition with friends. From what Dai Cin Er says, the danger of being killed by bandits is no less than that of being eaten by wolves or bitten by scorpions. But both pale compared to the desert itself. The way is dusty, with numerous flies and other insects, and little water. Prices for goods are high in the few oasis.

Still, the route is traveled. No doubt if we took some goods we'd offset some of the expenses. It is said a *jin* of silk will fetch a *jin* of gold in the western empire. But is it worth the risk?

Year 200 April 5

To our amazement, about a month ago, the Wood and Earth stars joined in heaven a third time. My colleagues were persuaded, and we set out as quickly as we could purchase camels and goods.

The road leads northwest through Lanzhou, curves north of the Mukden Depression—where nothing can live—hugs the foothills of the Mountains of Heaven, then heads southwest across a high pass into dry and hilly country. Dai, who will come as guide and translator, explained this to me. Goods are transported in relays; few travel its entire 12000 *li* length.* Towns in oasis along the way will make their living from us, as will the flies and mosquitoes.

Year 201 January 15

I've been unable to write. Every day is exhausting. Heat saps the life from my body, and there's never enough to drink. The earth here crunches under our feet, and mountains of strange "singing sand" thundered in yesterday's gale. It was like my trip to the ocean with my father in the typhoon season when I was a child. This morning we also heard wolves on the hunt. Worse, bandits have attacked several caravans before us. Our food runs low. Nevertheless, we feel as Master Kong said, "What can these things do to us until we have fulfilled our destiny?" Whatever waits for us at the end of the road, has somehow laid its grip on our hearts.

*4,000 miles

Year 201   March 29

A week ago we arrived in the city of Dun Huang. A caravan of dark-skinned men came to our inn a few days later, from south of the Taklimakan desert. They were dressed in strange robes. We talked far into the night.

I greatly enjoyed the conversation. They are men of learning; a pleasant change from the traders we meet so often on the road. (Yet, to tell the truth, I am hoping as much as those foul-mouthed movers of silk to gain something at the end of the road—a gift that will outweigh the ingots in my saddlebags in value as Mt. Tai outweighs them in jin.) The Southerners talked of the suffering living things endure. How well I have learned that these months! "The cause of suffering is desire," one told me. Certainly that is the cause of my troubles! And the Taklimakan desert yawns like a mouth before us. Its very name means "Go in and you'll never come out." This story of the king who found his way out of the desert by giving up all he owned moved me.

Maybe I would have turned left at the fork and sought his country. But the following evening the greatest marvel yet met our eyes. A new star arose, brighter than any in the sky.

Year 201   May 11

The guest star leads us west. When I close my eyes against the glare of the sun, I see it.

The desire within me has conquered the desert. It is like my thirst for a cool spring after the sun heats the sand all day, or like my wedding night. And yet it surpasses these, in its calm strength, and I don't know what I can say about it. Only this: if the wealth of Qin and the wisdom of Wen were set before me, I would choose this desert sand under my feet.

Yet I do not feel I am "grasping" as our friends on the way put it. I feel as if Heaven had its hands on me. There are days when I am "empty" of all but the trail, and I curse the flies and dust. But come evening, when the guest star rises bright in the West, my heart races. The pain is real, but it isn't that which keeps me awake long after I lie down, watching our guide move across the skies.

A question drives me on, more like a hunger than a thought. What will we find beyond these sands?

A Nation Called To Give *Fu* To The World

What would Chinese visitors have found in ancient Israel? A small country lush and green compared to much they'd traveled over. A nation that held as great a sense of its place in the world as China.

Perhaps they prepared themselves by reading the Jews' sacred writings along the road. If they had, they would have found the Jews were a people who not only loved life, but could have justified the Chinese idea of *Fu* theologically.

The oldest Jewish writing, *Genesis*, is translated thus in Chinese:

"So *Shang Di* created man in his own image, in the image of *Shang Di* he created him; male and female he created them. *Shang Di* gave them *Fu* and said to them, 'Be fruitful and increase in number; fill the earth and subdue it. Rule over the fish of the sea and the birds of the air and over every living creature that moves on the earth. . . *Shang Di* saw all things He had made, and it was very good."[3]

Every object on this planet, then, was given by the hand of the Creator and was "good."

The travelers would have found in the Jewish writings many truths to which their own language points. To begin with, the character *Fu* itself depicts the *Genesis* story of Creation.

On the left of *Fu* is *shen*, "God" or "gods."

On the right appear three radicals: *yi*, "one," *kou*, "mouth," and *tian*, "field." *Kou* is also a measure word: "five mouths" means "five animals or people."

福 The Chinese word *Fu* is a portrayal, then, of "One person in a garden next to God:" a succinct and vivid picture of Adam in the Garden of Eden.

From the very first, the Hebrew Scriptures related, God poured out material blessing on mankind. He provided the first man with every plant and animal, and all the land he could use. Fresh wonders met Adam every morning: the dawn reflected off lakes never before seen by human eyes, the new leaves of a willow tree, the first call of a mocking bird. Recently, an American Buddhist who converted to Christianity told me how the doctrine of creation re-awoke in him the wonder he once found in nature as a child.

Ecological balance and sanity shine from these pages. *Genesis* depicts the godly not just developing gardens and ruling the beasts, but also caring for the environment and rescuing animals from extinction. On the other hand, God seemed to agree that "having money is better than not," for *Genesis* says He put gold nearby the garden, to be dug out by the hand of man.

Everything Heaven made was "good." Matter wasn't an ugly illusion, but healthy and beautiful. God's creation was spread like a banquet before the first man. There was nothing evil in it or any suggestion he should leave it alone. Only, like the courses at a banquet, or the radicals in a Chinese character, each pleasure needed to be taken in proper order and proportion.

One stroke was missing, though. The man was alone.

If Buddha or some Christians had their say, he would have stayed that way. As Thomas Howard pointed out, if God had asked many religious people, they might not have thought it a good idea to create mankind in two sexes with a "great urge for each others' bodies."[4]

But God blessed the human race with sex, too.

Happiness Is Not Being Single

"The Lord God said, 'It is not good for man to be alone'. . . .
Then the Lord God made a woman."[5]

Here too the wise men might have noticed their own language had allied itself with the sacred texts of this little land. The character for "marital bliss," as we have mentioned, is formed by the joining of two "joy" characters. Several other characters drive the point home.

The Chinese word for "palace" shows two mouths under one roof. 宮 "Companion" is formed with the person radical and two mouths. 吕 "Flesh" is made by putting two people in an enclosure: 肉 It is as if this character were invented to illustrate in pictographic short-hand what the account of Adam and Eve concludes about marriage: "They will be one flesh."

The word peace, too, by which the capitals of both China and Israel were named (and also an old name for Beijing), reflect the wisdom of monogamy. 安 shows one woman, 女 , under a roof. 宀 Polygamists have proven that more than one woman under one roof is not the path to peace. Some religious pilgrims have shown it is possible, by leaving home, to obtain a coward's cease-fire in the battle of the sexes. But when it comes to sex, Chinese language hinted at a more sensible "Middle Way." And the prophets of Israel were the spur that drove the world to accept this path as the best form in which to funnel human sexuality.

The word for "unfaithfulness," 姦 , on the other hand, shows three little "female" forms, like the wives of a respected and traditional Chinese merchant or petty official. Again, rather than affirming what Chinese emperors and heros normally practiced, the wisdom encoded in the Chinese language comes down on the side of Biblical truth.

As this last character hints, an affirmation of instinct was not enough for Israel any more than it had been for China. The human tendency is to grasp too much or scorn it all, drink through the night and curse at our bellies the next day, abuse our lovers and then complain when "the thrill is gone." All problems of both sorts, said the prophets, originally arose from the attempt to base ultimate happiness on something other than fellowship with God.

The first man and women learned to grasp. God did not leave them because they enjoyed His creation. Rather, they left Him to enjoy things in their own way and in their own sweet time. Like the prodigal son, mankind veered from the way of true happiness and soon found itself knawing on stale bread crusts, thinking of home.

Because of this, every step towards fullness must involve an emptying. We cut ourselves off from God, and until that rift is healed, every good thing becomes a danger to our souls.

Israel, like China, waited for someone to bridge the gap.

Promises Of A Cure

Soon after the creation story and the story of how human happiness was shattered, the book of Genesis introduced a man named Abraham, who lived in what is today Iraq.

God told Abraham also to go west into the desert. On the far side, He promised, He would bring a blessing not just to one man, but ultimately for all people. In Chinese that promise reads:

> "I will give you *Fu*. . . I will make you *Fu*. . . I will give *Fu* to those who give you *Fu* and curse those who curse you. . . And all the peoples on earth will get *Fu* because of you."[6]

Unlike the stories of Buddha, a threat is included in the promise. In a world where mothers sell daughters and police take bribes, where war criminals retire in luxury after a lifetime of causing misery, is this so surprising? Even to straighten a leg, a doctor causes pain. When the divine friendship that makes for true happiness has been shattered by sin, would we not be fooling ourselves to look for a painless cure?

But sometimes, as the myths of China's story-tellers and the ideals of her great teachers implied, and as the journey of the wise men showed, a good man might take a curse on himself so blessing might fall on others. This also was the hope of Israel.

About the time Confucius looked out from Mt. Tai, Isaiah penned these words:

> "The people who walked in darkness have seen a great light; on those who live in the land of the shadow of death a light has shown."[7]

This "light" wouldn't strike only the land of Israel:

"I will also make you a light to the Gentiles, so you may bring my salvation to the far reaches of the earth."[8]

Again echoing Chinese language and culture, "good" would come through a woman with an infant:

"For unto us a child is born, unto us a son is given. . ."

But this child would be from Heaven.

"His name will be called Wonderful Counsellor, Mighty God, Everlasting Father, Prince of Peace. . . "[9]

The price he would pay to redeem us would be high.

"He is despised and forsaken of men, a man of sorrows, and acquainted with grief. . . He was wounded for our transgressions, he was bruised for our iniquities; the punishment for our well-being fell on him, and with his stripes we are healed."[10]

Cured of cancer, this believer now prays for the sick and preaches the Gospel in nearby towns.

Frank and Annie Bartellato pray God's blessing on a newly-wed couple. The groom was a drug addict who recovered at Agape Fellowship.

The Stable At The End Of The World

The astronomers came to a rough dug-out in a Bethlehem hillside, where they found a mother with a child. His name, the father told them perhaps a bit shyly, was Jesus—"Savior." Except for one donkey, the livestock milling around didn't belong to this poor but proud family. The wise men gave them gold and other gifts, and the parents accepted gladly. They were very poor.

Confucius presented the theme of this new life when he said "It may be that a righteous man will have to die." Guan Yin, Miao Shan and Lei Feng drew sketches of his life on China's imagination. This life would reveal better than any the paradox of the Silk Road.

Jewish novelist Sholem Asch wrote,

"Everything He ever said or did has value for us today, and that is something you can say of no other man, alive or dead."[11]

The world waited for a Savior. Even now, his birthday is the most anticipated event of the year in most the world. His words and deeds brought unique blessing to mankind, even in this life.

Why, then, is the religion Jesus founded represented by a cross, an instrument of torture and death?

Joseph, after his exhausting labor, leading a pregnant wife across the country, could have answered this question. Mary, who endured a controversial pregnancy, a long trip and childbirth, knew the answer too. The wise men had also found the answer to this question.

A gift is only as precious as the price that is paid for it—not in cash, but in tears, sweat and blood.

****

Accounts say Jesus fed thousands of people on a few fish and loaves of bread. These stories are often questioned, and in the next chapter we will consider whether they are believable. What can't be questioned is that his teachings have inspired millions to similar acts. In his name, followers take food and development aid around the world. Christians have also made many of the contributions to science that help poor countries feed themselves.

Yet Jesus shut his ears to the calls of his own stomach for food for forty days and nights, so that he could pray.

Jesus' first miracle was to make a wedding more *"renao"* by changing water into wine. He made the act of love more meaningful, not only by making cheap sex taboo, but also by choosing romance as a symbol to describe his love for the Church. Yet he refused this pleasure for himself.

Jesus traveled everywhere with friends. Yet he would often slip away to be alone with God. In his hour of greatest need, he was even more alone. The masses turned on him. His disciples deserted him. Even God seemed absent from the universe.

Those who desired long life and health in ancient Israel came to Jesus. At his touch, the Gospels say, the blind saw. Paraplegics were cured. Madmen regained clarity of mind. The dead came to life.

Hospitals founded in Jesus' name can be found almost everywhere there are sick people. The world praises Mother Teresa, but I have met hundreds of Christians like her in Asia, feeding and bathing street people, rescuing prostitutes, looking after orphans, digging fish ponds for refugees, planting macadamia nuts for tribal people.

A University of Hong Kong report found one Christian drug center to be ten times as successful as government centers. A study of an inner-city mission in America yielded an almost identical comparison. I've met these people. I've talked with Chinese who were addicted to heroin or amphetamine in Taiwan, Hong Kong and Thailand, who overcame their chemical craving when they came to Jesus.

Jesus was not passive or indifferent about life. As the "Great Physician," he loved life more than anyone, and "sweat drops of blood" the night before his death.[12]

So much life flowed from this one man's hands. Yet those hands were nailed to a cross.

Jesus warned those who wanted to follow him that they, too, would go through the desert.

An intellectual from Taiwan found two groups of people becoming Christians in mainland China:

"Some intellectuals pursue (the Christian) faith because it's 'useful' in saving the Chinese nation and awakening sleepy consciences. Some people in their eagerness to benefit the people, upset that the people stubbornly refuse to awake, want to enlist God in the struggle."

He admired rural believers more:

"The life of the peasants is relatively harsh. . . Having nothing else to depend on, they often pray to Buddha and the gods. Christian preachers who come to the countryside bring a supernatural power to heal the sick and cast out devils, making the people believe that Jesus Christ is the true God through incidents they see with their own eyes and hear with their own ears. Peasants see face to face that Jesus is more powerful than other gods, and worship him as the true God."[13]

I've met both classes of Christian in China. Intellectuals have told me how they chose poverty or even prison to bring Christ's love to China. Peasants from Anhui and Zhejiang have told me how they cast out demons and healed the sick in his name. Teenage girls run from town to town one step ahead of Public Security. Young men study theology in smoky caves and survive on rice and bean sprouts. Old men suffer cruel beatings. Middle-aged men give up good businesses to preach, in an age when China smolders with desire for money.

Whether to benefit China, or to benefit a neighbor, each follows Jesus across his or her own Silk Road. Why? "There is a God-shaped vacuum" in the human heart, said Pascal. To be filled, we must first become empty. Thus poverty is the way to riches. Chastity is the road to happy and fulfilling marriage. Those who die to themselves will live in Christ, for the desert is the route to paradise.

Blessing begins when "one mouth in a garden draws near to God," but it never ends there. Just as a mother robin's mouth opens to give what it once opened to receive, so the follower of Christ blesses others by "dying to self." But after death comes new life.

This is the story of the Gospels. It is a beautiful, painful, challenging story. It fulfills many hints in Chinese characters, mythology and even commercial history. It also moves the deepest hopes and fears in our hearts. Like the wise men, while reading it we feel not that we are trying to grasp Heaven, but that it somehow has laid hold on us.

But can we trust this story? Some say the Gospels, like the tales monks brought from India about Avalokitsvara, are just a myth, important for the moral of the tale, rather than for the historical facts of Jesus life. Let us see.

Chapter Ten

Is Jesus Another Guan Yin Myth?

The shore of the Sea of Galilee in Israel is dotted with fishing villages. Life on the water has always had hazards, since the lake is subject to sudden high winds. If you believe the *Gospels*, about two thousand years ago it was subject to miracles, too: people walking on water, sudden huge catches of fish, gale-force winds that suddenly died to nothing and waves that fell flat like glass. The surrounding area, too, witnessed surprising and powerful shifts of the cosmic wind in favor of local residents. Blind men suddenly saw. A little girl who died came to life. Lame men walked. A woman who had an ulcer for twelve years regained her health. All these events and many more were somehow bound up with the comings and goings of a remarkably wise but controversial young teacher.

Even many who followed him, say the *Gospels*, couldn't believe their eyes. But in the modern era scholars claim the authority of science to reject the supernatural works of Jesus.

The Gospel miracles are "legends," wrote the scholar Thomas Sheehan, "projected backwards under the impact of faith into the life of the historical Jesus."[1] John Collins of Notre Dame University called the quieting of the Galilean surf "theological fiction."[2] Rabbi Roland Gittelsohn described passages in which Jesus fulfilled prophecy as "propaganda" written "a generation to a generation and a half" after the facts.[3]

American magazines like *Time* and *Atlantic Monthly* have followed the lead of these scholars with cover articles on the "historical Jesus." If you'd lived by the Sea of Galilee in the First Century, the articles within implied, life would have proven tamer than the *Gospels* say. Storms would have risen and fallen with the prevailing winds. The blind stayed blind, and the dead, dead. As for the charismatic young teacher, Jesus. . . . It seems he was a sagacious young radical who stirred up some scientifically-preliterate peasants. As the years passed, his disciples garbled and exaggerated his deeds. One gathering of scholars called the *Jesus Seminar* voted on Jesus' ethical teachings: the few which were his, and the greater portion, which they say got thrown into the mix by later enthusiasts.

The critics' theories have spread to every corner of the world, including China. Teachers of various faiths eagerly but uncritically seize upon these ideas, perhaps to outflank the threat a True Son of Heaven might bring to their pre-set ideologies. Secular leaders say, "Jesus must after all have been just a good man who got in trouble for teaching humanitarianism." Marxists, even more skeptical, say, "If the man ever lived, he was a revolutionary." Buddhists, too, put a typical spin on the doubts of the critics. "As a Buddhist I say values are more important than flesh-and-blood facts," one wrote. "If people say he existed, then he existed, because the lessons of life that we are told about are important indeed."[4]

But most of us do care about "flesh-and-blood facts," and people, too. We never placed that much hope in these abstract ideologies. We were looking for a Savior who would save flesh-and-blood beings like ourselves. If Jesus is just another Guan Yin myth, what do we need him for? And so many, intimidated by the arguments of the ideologists, slipped back into despair.

But is it really the "scientific method" which doubts the Gospels? Or is it just the irrational fears of a few scholars who read more than they see, and guess more than they read?

Are the miracles of Jesus myths, like those of Miao Shan, or even propaganda, like that of Lei Feng? Should we lay the Gospel to rest as just another Guan Yin tale, a wishful dream of a Savior who never was?

Or is it the doubts of these skeptics we should drop?

I opt for the latter. With the help of a few fairy tales, a calendar, and the *Analects* of Confucius, let me explain why.

First, let us look at the literary form of the Gospels.

Placing Gospels On The Library Shelf

One day I bought a couple books in Kunming's Foreign Language Bookstore. The first was a collection of Grimm's fairy tales. The second, *Dragon Tales*, was an assortment of short stories about mortals who have adventures with *long*, what the West calls dragons. I settled in my hotel room to read.

114

Mysterious old men guided soldiers out of the clutch of an enemy, then vanished in a fog. Mortals seeded clouds with tears till storms flooded their homes. Wicked witches lived in gingerbread houses; black dragons inhabited underground palaces. Young people went on quests. Dogs were people who were dragons.

One was the product of European culture, the other of Chinese. One spoke of fairies, the other of dragons. But I hardly felt, as I moved from one book to the other, that I needed a passport. I had made it to the country where dreams and nightmares come from. I was developing a cold, and after a while the episodes in each took on qualities of mild delirium, with their strange creatures and grotesque but poetic magic.

An allegory is a very different sort of story. The most popular tall tales in Chinese and English—*The Journey to the West*, and *Pilgrim's Progress*—belong to this category. The first is almost as light-hearted as *Alice in Wonderland*, with monkeys and demons in place of rabbits and mad hatters. The second, following the tradition of *Odyssey*, is more sober. *Journey* and *Progress* were written hundreds of years and thousands of miles apart, and obviously in different moods. Yet the quest, heroism, swashbuckling adventure, magic and symbolic meaning, mark them as belonging to the same category of imaginative work.

If we are to call the miracles of Jesus fiction, with which set of stories should we place them? The *Gospels* have been called legend, myth, allegory, hoax, and propaganda. But they clearly do not belong to any known form of fiction.

A.N.Wilson, the skeptical English biographer, admitted in *Jesus, a Life,*

> "You could go to a library in the ancient world and find histories, letters, biographies (of a sort), prose fiction, epic verse, drama, philosophical dialogues, mathematics, magic, and medicine. But you could not find any other 'Gospels.' They are a unique literary genre."[5]

The most famous of the skeptical scholars, Rudolf Bultmann, went as far as to say,

> "The analogies that are to hand serve only to throw the uniqueness of the Gospel into still stronger relief."[6]

C. S. Lewis, teacher at Cambridge and Oxford Universities and one of the best-read scholars of his generation, wrote of the *Gospel of John,*

"I have been reading poems, romances, vision-literature legends, myths all my life. I know what they are like. I know that not one of them is like this." [7]

The power of God: recovering drug addicts at a Christian Center in Thailand.

What Are Gospels Like?

The miracles of Jesus, in contrast to fictional magic, are prosaic, reasonable, and even understated. People reacted to them like we would if we'd been there, or like we know people commonly react to great deeds by great men. Some were bowled over. "'What kind of man is this?' They said, 'Even the wind and the waves obey him!'"[8] Others were frightened. Party functionaries wanted to use Jesus for political purposes. Still others reacted in anger or disbelief. Rivals claimed Jesus was relying on powers of darkness. Religious fanatics plotted his assassination.

In the *Gospels* you feel a mounting tension and drama, like in a biography of Sun Yat-Sen or Mahatma Gandhi. The difference is, this time it isn't the message, it is the identify of the messenger, that stokes the fire. Yet the *Gospels* are anything but strident. They are written in (as German scholar Cartem Thiede said of Matthew): "A very sober, concise, unembellished Greek, correct, pared to the bone." [9]

The closest parallel I can think of is the *Analects* of Confucius. The *Analects*, like the *Gospels*, consist of sayings and deeds of a teacher that disciples later wrote down and collected, taking pain to let the words and actions of their Master speak for themselves. The problem of judging historical reliability is also similar.

What Did Confucius Say?

Most everyone agrees Confucius actually said most of what the *Analects* claim he said. H. G. Creel said "virtually all" scholars agree the first half of the *Analects*, especially, are highly reliable.

Why? First, Creel wrote,

"One of the best evidences of its authenticity is the fact that, while the *Analects* is obviously a Confucian book, it contains much that Confucius would have preferred that it did not include."[10]

The examples Creel gave were "squabbles between the disciples," a disciple who questioned the greatness of Confucius, and the fact that Confucius is shown talking with an immoral woman. ("This has embarrassed countless prudish Confucians.")

But in none of these details are the *Analects* nearly as frank as the *Gospels*. Jesus was "a friend of sinners." The *Gospels* show him scandalously doing dinner with the dregs of society: quislings, radicals, and prostitutes. He developed a reputation for hanging out with shady characters.

Disbelief, criticism, and even cynicism are the backdrop against which Jesus worked his miracles. John the Baptist doubted if Jesus "was he, or should we wait for another?"[11] The *Gospels* never tell us if he resolved his doubts. Religious leaders said Jesus was "out of his mind" and in cahoots with the devil.[12] The disciples ran away when Jesus was arrested. Their leader, Peter, denied he even knew his Master!

Is this flattery? Is this hagiography? What we find in the *Gospels* is clearly not the work of a pious forger. No biography is more ruthlessly true to unpleasant facts.

Not only do the *Gospels* bare every mark of honesty, they have a tremendous advantage over the *Analects* and every other ancient record anywhere in the world: there are four of them.

Some make much of differences among the *Gospels*. Did Peter see one angel or two? Did Jesus cure one blind man, or two? What is striking though is not the disagreements—we expect perspectives to differ—but the agreements. I began to count details in the *Gospel of John* that confirm the other three, and found several dozen in the first three chapters alone.

A building that rests on four pillars isn't just four times as strong as one built on a single pillar. It's hundreds of times stronger. An attorney with four witnesses who agree as much as the *Gospels* will sleep well at night.

That is—and here's the rub—if they really were close to the events they claim to describe.

Some say the people who saw Jesus were no longer alive by the time his biographers went to work. Skeptics imply this when they talk about "material of the tradition" being "preserved and transmitted," as if talking about the evolution of the horse. Kerry Temple, editor of *Notre Dame Magazine*, said the *Gospels* "did not take shape until a generation after Jesus died"[(13)]— and who knows how the truth might be distorted after all those years. Rabbi Gittelsohn, following the lead of radical scholars from the last century, said the Gospels were written a "generation to a century and a half after Jesus' death."[(14)]

Are the *Gospels* products of eyewitness testimony? Or were they written too long after the facts to trust?

Saving Time In Ceramic Jars

In the early 1960s, a fragment of a *Gospel of John*—which skeptics say was the last written—was found from the year 125 A.D. The *Gospels* could not, then, have been written "a century and a half" after the crucifixion, which would be 175 A.D.

Temple vaguely said the *Gospels* were compiled "late in the First Century." When he needed to give a specific date, he said 70 A.D.— just forty years after the storm on Galilee.[(15)] Cartem Thiede, examining pieces of a manuscript of *Matthew* preserved at Oxford, says those fragments are probably from about 70 A.D.[(16)]

The earliest copy of the *Analects* now available is a stone slab carved 750 years after Confucius. Chen Jing Pan says that "perhaps the best" and "comparatively most reliable" biography of Confucius is found in *Shi Qi* (Historical Records), compiled four hundred years after his death.[(17)] Creel feels that work is unreliable. But he calls the *Mencius*, written about 150 years after Confucius' death, a "very valuable source" for the life of the teacher.[(18)]

Forty years is not a long time. Especially considering the age of the disciples when their Master left them.

Mobile revolutionary movements attract young people. A disciple born in 10 A.D. would only be sixty years old by 70 A.D. My grandmother wrote poetry at 95 years of age. If she'd been one of Jesus' teenage followers, she could have edited an eyewitness account *four decades* after even radical scholars admit the *Gospels* were all done!

All this talk of generations fading from the earth and traditions being carelessly passed on sounds reasonable until you take a close look at the facts. But the truth is, the *Gospels* not only appear to be based on eyewitness accounts, there is no reason on earth they shouldn't have been. At the time the *Gospels* were written, I doubt you could have gone to any Jewish church east of Sicily without bumping into at least a few people who'd watched Jesus do miracles.

At this point some raise an opposite doubt. The *Gospels* appear too detailed, too realistic, too precise! Could witnesses really have remembered what they saw in their youth so well?

Recently an article written by Mao Tse Tung's personal physician appeared in *U.S.News and World Report*. He related what he saw as long as forty years before. He explained,

> "Because Mao's language was so colorful and vivid and deeply etched in my brain, I was able to recall verbatim much of what he said."[19]

No one spoke or acted in more striking terms than Jesus. If a famous man healed you of cancer and said "Now go and sin no more," or miraculously multiplied *mantou* before your hungry eyes and told you "Everything is possible for him who believes," would you ever forget it?

I've witnessed miracles, though few as dramatic as those in the *Gospels*. I may forget where I left my umbrella yesterday or what I had for breakfast this morning. But when it comes to those healings in northern Thailand and God's provision on the streets of Seattle and Taipei, I have instant, multi-sensual recall: the weather, the bugs that circled the lamps, the tone of people's voices even.

Of course the disciples remembered. How could they forget?

Why Doubters Doubt

Wilson was mystified over what happened at Jesus' grave site after his burial. How could a man write so beautifully about love as the author of *John*, yet tell a "whopping lie" like the Resurrection?

> "Since the story is untrue, palpably and obviously untrue, — bodies do not, in our kosmos, resurrect themselves—how do we reconcile ourselves to the paradox that the *New Testament* is patently the work of men striving to be good?"[20]

Being a literary man, Wilson looked for literary parallels.

Consider William Blake, he said. The great poet used in all sincerity to tell friends he'd been talking with angels, or had been visited by the prophet Isaiah. When the friends asked where his visitors had gone, Blake would "tap the side of his head."

Such comparisons only show up better how believable the *Gospels* are.

Blake's "miracles" were a piece with his poetry: personal, romantic, and highly imaginative. The *Gospels*, on the other hand, were public property, a deposition on events witnessed by thousands. Down-to-earth realism, dogged skepticism, even derision, are the background of nearly every scene.

Also, though by nature they were fearful men, the apostles gambled with their lives on the truth of what they witnessed, which Blake never did. What poetic dream or half-doubted vision of Guan Yin could have made Thomas or Peter endure torture and death and refuse to recant? Ten of Jesus' eleven apostles, besides many other eyewitnesses, died witnessing to Jesus' miracles. Did they all have an identical dream so real that each was willing to die for it?

Those who reply "But miracles just can't happen, they contradict science" are like the frog in the well in the Chinese proverb. Outside the narrow circle of their experience, miracles happen every day. A sick person was certainly healed in Jesus' name somewhere in the world in the last five minutes. They do not know the kosmos as well as they think; they only know one small corner of it. They should edge out from the cozy but claustrophobic confines of skepticism and "seek truth from facts," not impose their lack of experience on the universe.

Here, too, the world needs a true "Middle Way:" neither blind faith and superstition, nor blind skepticism. We need faith, but a faith that relies on evidence. As Jesus said, "Look at my hands. Reach out your arms and touch."[21]

The Sound of *Fu*

The documents of the New Testament were written by at least eight different people. Six claimed to be eyewitnesses to the miracles of Christ. The rest were a part of the milieu in which the sick continued to be healed and the dead raised.

Many people have made up stories about Jesus. All that I have read, except for the four orthodox Gospels, fit into preset and familiar patterns: apocryphal tales from the second century, propagandist tracts like the *Gospel of Barnabas*, the *Gospel of the Holy Twelve*, or the *Book of Mormon*.

Most are clearly frauds. The words of Jesus in the *Book of Mormon*, for instance, are a ponderous rehash of *New Testament* sayings in pseudo-King James English.

The *National Review* called the words of Jesus "inimitable," saying by comparison even Shakespeare is "shallow stuff." Fyodor Dostoevsky's fictional masterpiece, the *Brothers Kharamazov*, which has been called the "Fifth Gospel," shows this truth. The high point of his book is the short story the *Grand Inquisitor*, in which Jesus is interrogated by a Spanish bishop. In that story, Jesus said not a word. I suspect Dostoevsky knew, if he tried to put words in Jesus' mouth, the illusion he had built of his presence would collapse.

Not only are there no other *Gospels* in all of world literature, no other person like Jesus of Nazareth has ever appeared among us. In all history, only here do we see a believable portrait of Heaven come in the shape of man. Like at the top of Mt. Tai, anything human lips try to add, only shatters our sense of God's presence.

Is The Box Empty Or Full?

When they despair of convincing people that the disciples made up the *Gospels*, many critics try an opposite tactic. "The *Gospels* are clearly testimonies of faith, written by people who believe to persuade other people to believe," they say. "How can we believe the disciples? They had an agenda."

Of course they did. That is why I trust them. It is clear to me the *Gospels* were written by people who were certain of the historical facts, and intended to make me sure too.

Yet in one sense the skeptics are right when they say the *Gospels* resemble myths. A myth is truth which echoes fears and wishes that sleep in the shadows of the mind. In these records, dreams step boldly into the light and walk under the sun of first century Palestine.

The world has spent its evenings chasing shadows: Guan Yin, Miao Shan, Lei Feng, Psyche, Mithras. Even fairy tales like *Beauty and the Beast* and *Little Mermaid* move readers with a pattern of paradise lost through neglect, future hope, and the redemptive power of sacrificial love. Could it be that in the streets of Bethlehem the wise men really came to a patch of ground where "The hopes and fears of all the years" met?

I have given a few reasons why I believe the "Sounds of *Fu*" are not myth, but fact. I believe Confucius would have recognized Jesus as the "holy man" who brings the benevolence of Heaven to earth. I think anyone who honestly considers the *Gospels* will come to the same conclusion.

It is understandable if some find the salvation God provides in Jesus "Too good to be true." The disciples themselves sometimes couldn't believe their eyes. Almost every believer at some point asks, "Am I deceiving myself? Suppose it's a delusion after all?" Each of us needs to honestly face such questions.

But much skepticism is dishonest. Some doubt for the sake of doubt, or because they don't really want God to be part of their happiness. They would rather substitute gold, or wisdom, or love of humanity.

Some would rather not walk the desert. Others are determined to find their own path across it.

****

Buddha warned against grasping *Fu*. But it seems to me there is also the danger of holding on to emptiness.

A woman received a gift from the man she admired. She took one look at it, and put it on the top shelf of her cupboard. "Oh, the wrapping is so lovely!" She sighed. "But how can there be anything inside? And if there is, I'll have to worry about keeping the dust off and protecting it from robbers. We may even get married, but our love will fade some day and the children will leave home. I will keep the box unopened and treasure it forever as a symbol of that which I can never possess."

Her words represent a kind of wisdom. Only inside the box is an engagement ring from one who truly loves her.

The *Gospels* contain a gift from God. Why do some leave this gift unopened? In many ways, the fear to open up, or to go inside, is natural, and even healthy. We will see in the final section how a wise caution about carelessly crossing frontiers is reflected in the time-tested wisdom of China. But Chinese walls, gates, and graveyards also prepare us in a unique and wonderful way to enter into the love God offers in Jesus.

The shadow of a church's cross falls
on a peacock, local symbol of
renewed life in southern China.

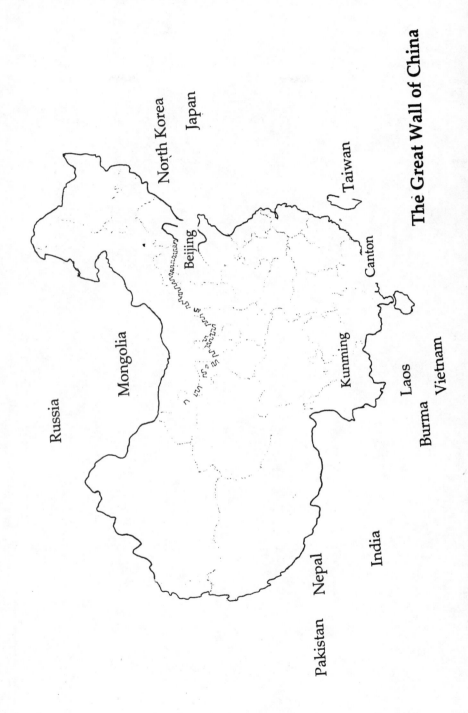

The Great Wall of China

門
Part IV
Inside The Gate

Once built to keep people out, the Great Wall now
attracts people from all over the world to China.

Above: the old way.
Below: the new way.
"Spring in the motherland."

Chapter Eleven

Spooks, Bandits, and Power Saws

"Foreigners aren't allowed in provincial buildings." A soldier in green fatigues and cap with red star explained, pointing to a little one-story building to the right of the gate. "Come inside the guardhouse and someone will come down to meet you."

I glanced past the gate again at the half-Soviet half-Romanesque architecture of the Yunnan government buildings. It looked like this would be the closest I'd get. Then I followed the soldier into a small building just to the right and on the outside of the gate.

A short, matronly woman stared incredulously at me. As a foreigner, I'd gotten used to attracting attention, usually friendly. So I looked back. At first glance I thought she must be someone's grandmother. That's what Little Red Riding Hood thought about the wolf.

"Who is this?" She asked the guards. She turned to me. "Get out of here! What are you doing here? Go on, get out!" I looked at the guards. They seemed hard of hearing.

"Go! Get! You leave right NOW!" She yelled, then turned back to the soldiers. "Why did you let a foreigner in here by the provincial buildings? Foreigners have AIDS."

I sat down and tried to collect my thoughts and dignity. As a matter of fact, I had come to talk about AIDS—how to keep it from spreading to China. I was part of the solution, not part of the problem. Maybe if I explained to the soldiers they'd quiet the elderly lady down? But when I brought the subject of AIDS up again she stormed even more, demanding the men in green get rid of me.

127

What was inside the gate? What secrets did "Grandma Wolf" want to keep from the outside world? I hoped they'd invite me in.

****

One of the first things a visitor notices in China is walls. It is said the Great Wall is the easiest man-made object to make out from space. Smaller walls guard buildings, parks, monuments, temples, and graves.

The walls China builds in the face of the outside world often affect visitors as those at the Yunnan government buildings affected me.

From the time Kublai Khan sent Marco Polo to scout the country for him, merchants, missionaries and explorers have pushed on whatever doors China left closed. Even today, you hear dialogues like this among young travelers:

"How far did you get?"

"I went through remote areas where I didn't see another foreigner for three weeks. I saw incredible mountains and met minority people who wore bizarre rings. I didn't have any problems until the police fined me in the last village."

The first person may ask how to get to this hidden Shangri La. Or he may tell his own story. When Tibet is closed "I made it to Llasa" is the royal flush of travelers' boasts.

What are they smoking? A loaded question
along the Burmese border in Yunnan Province.

There is something about going "where no outsider has gone before" that makes my pulse race, too. I visited a patch of towering mountains and deep tropical valleys along the Vietnam border that left me with haunting memories. They tasted all the more poignant when someone told me I was the first American to visit since a pilot was shot down there during the Vietnam War. It was like making the first tracks across fresh snow.

That's what China's doors look like from the outside.

Of all peoples, the Chinese may know best what doors look like from the inside. China is a country that put itself behind a wall, after all. Not without good reason.

Knocking On The Great Wall

Every Chinese defines who he is by which doors he sees from within and which from without. The character 內 ("nei") is a picture of this: a man 人 inside an enclosure 冂 . Outside 外 ("wai") is easy for foreigners to learn. Children often point at them and shout "wai guo ren" ("out-country-person") or "lao wai" ("old out"). I've also heard "old white," "out-person," and once in a long while the more insulting "foreign devil," or in Hong Kong, "old devil."

Before the 19th Century, most "outside country people" came to China across the Silk Road. China built the Great Wall facing the deserts of Central Asia to keep out those who were not wanted.

The Great Wall was the world's most impressive construction project. It is seven to eight meters high, six to seven meters thick at the base and about five at the top. Its five thousand kilometer length still writhes like a dragon across the tops of mountains from the Yellow Sea to Gansu Province: as long as from San Francisco to Miami and up to New York.

The Wall is actually many walls, some joined, some ruined and lost, some mounds just detectable under centuries of sod like the work of an ancient race of moles. Twenty different dynasties and principalities worked on various stages of the Wall. Emperor Qin drove nearly two million workers; mostly convicts who'd fallen afoul of some regulation or regulator, to chip stone and haul mortar in irons. Then he garrisoned his white-picket fence with a million soldiers. As I sat on the Wall at Badaling near Beijing one day, even with thousands of tourists the wall seemed forlorn. At night, Mongolian winds sighing across its heavy stone: even with a million soldiers it must have seemed a lonely place.

What was the point of such a stupendous investment of manpower? Simple. To keep foreigners out.

A monument to paranoia? Not if you consider the folk on the other side of the Wall. Around China's vast frontiers whirled nomadic herdsmen, the ancestors of Ghenghis Khan's soldiers, swift on horseback and quick with arrow. They might climb a wall, but their horses couldn't. Then there were tribes in the south who came down to Chinese homesteads to hunt heads with which to placate the gods at spring planting, or to drag slaves back to mountain strongholds. Later the English and Japanese came from the sea, no more trustworthy and much better-armed.

China sees walls as the defense of the civilized against the savage. The Great Wall, like "Closed Door" policies of later emperors, were attempts to protect the Middle Kingdom from barbarism.

China will never forget what happened when the Wall was breached: the Mongol and Manchu conquests or the massacres in Nanjing and other cities during World War Two.

But the bitterest memory of all came at the hands of Europeans. In the 1840s the British, with help from the French, laid waste to the Chinese coast and forced China to import opium from Britain's Indian colonies. For a century after that humiliation, gaunt addicts wandered China's back alleys. It was her Waterloo and Stalingrad, her "trail of tears," the height of her national disgrace. A gang of "outside country people" had forced the gate, and it felt like rape.

China hasn't forgotten, or quite forgiven. And yet few Chinese ask whether Tibet or Korea might have similar complaints against China's military actions in the past forty years.

The lady I met at the guardhouse was no doubt raised on stories of western imperialism. It's a wonder to me there are so few like her in China today. At the time of my visit a new "opium war" was brewing a few hundred miles away. Hundreds of thousands of young Chinese men were discovering a chemically-induced nirvana. The drugs were crossing the border. At least three hundred smugglers were shot in Yunnan within a few months; later I watched a couple more paraded away on a flatbed truck near Burma. The Chinese press warned ominously: "Foreign drug dealers are involved!" The fact that this time the drugs were coming directly from fellow-Asians, and allies at that, was easy to lose sight of.

Was the white man standing by the gate to blame? Maybe not personally. If not him, it was some other "*waiguoren*."

A More Open China Awaits. . . What?

But China is changing. Unreasoning fear of outsiders is slowly on the wane. For some, it's been replaced by uncritical acceptance: some young people take American tycoons, or Madonna or Michael Jackson, as a model for the good life.

Were a Mongolian Don Quixote to come to Badaling Pass, he'd find the Wall defended by a strike force of international tourists. The "canons" they point through gaps in the wall only shoot pictures. He'd even find Colonel Sanders, hand stretched out in friendship, on the Mongolian side of the pass.

"A more open China awaits the 2000 Olympics," signs all over Beijing read while the nation was wooing the millennial sports meet in 1992. China's leaders see the world has changed. Foreigners come with credit card and basketball, not sword and gun.

But foreigners also bring dangerous ideas, and not just democracy or high-tech. Outsiders also bring the thrill of drugs, of easy sex and fast living. And yes, a little peninsula of Chinese territory that stretches into Burma by 1992 contained three quarters of China's AIDS cases, contracted from shooting *foreign* drugs.

The planet is smaller than it was fifty years ago, and China has come to realize she must be part of it. Communism doesn't join China to anyone but a few cranky demi-gods in backwaters like Cuba and North Korea. The Chinese need a door by which they can meet the world as brothers under Heaven, yet retain the identity of their unique culture and protect themselves from bandits.

The Little Walls Of China

Some of China's tallest walls were built to keep out Chinese.

"Inside person" (内人) means "wife" in Chinese. No gap is as stark to China as that between family members and the rest of the human race.

Tourists who don't have the chance to visit Chinese in their homes sometimes leave China with a bad impression of how people treat each other. Passengers trample one another to get on a bus. Waiters talk with friends and drink tea while customers wait to order. On passenger ships, people smoke and shout and play cards all night while people try to sleep a few feet away.

On my last trip to China, a woman sitting next to me on a train held her baby up to urinate in the aisle. Then she handed her baby to an elderly lady next to her and sat down alone. I looked at the pool of urine at my feet and asked, "Would you mind cleaning it up?" "It doesn't matter," She answered.

Sometimes the feelings of strangers don't seem to matter much in China.

But at a friend's home, you meet a different side of the Chinese character. Your hosts may spend a week's salary to buy the food, and slave all day over a fiery wok to titillate your tongue. They purchase expensive cuts of meat. They fill your glass with their best alcohol, and place the tastiest morsels on your bowl of rice. They wine and dine you, tell you how good your Chinese is (even if it isn't), send you home with what's left, and insist you come back soon.

Bill Holms' experience with one poor family along the Yangtse River has been shared to one extent or another by many humbled foreigners:

> "I visit people with an income of less than thirty dollars a month, living in a one-room apartment with a dirt floor, no car, no heat, no flush toilet, no running water, no kitchen, not much electricity, two or three changes of clothes, and a wall full of books. I eat them out of house and home for four or five days, am entertained grandly, not allowed to spend a fen, and for the pleasure of bankrupting them, they give me elegant gifts. . ."[1]

Sometimes you meet people whose friendship comes with strings, who want to "pull relations," to work their friendship with you for some advantage. But more often, a invitation to a Chinese home is a ticket to a wonderful experience of sincere hospitality and friendship.

Chinese cities also have a clearly-defined "inside" and "outside." Over most of her turbulent history China's cities and villages have been vulnerable to outlaws and to the predatory armies of war lords. Each town carefully maintained and defended a perimeter wall. Jung Chang described the wall around one small city in north China:

> "Yixian was build like a fortress. It was encircled by walls thirty feet high and twelve feet thick. . . surmounted by battlements, dotted with sixteen forts at regular intervals, and wide enough to ride a horse quite easily along the top. There were four gates into the city, one at each point of the compass, with outer protecting gates, and the fortifications were surrounded by a deep moat."[2]

Imagine a visitor's thoughts as he rode up to such a town as the sun slipped below hills on the horizon. Would the gate be open? Would he be welcomed in? Or left outside for the night—with thieves and wolves from those mountains?

From inside different questions had to be asked. Who is this stranger? Is it safe to let him in?

Most colleges in China are also surrounded by high brick walls, often with sharp glass laid along the top. You may need to come in by the front gate, past a guard. Sometimes you have to register or prove you have business. Who are you? What is your "*dan wei* (Work unit)"? At one school where I studied, guards were strict with Chinese visitors because a rapist or murderer was rumored to be stalking the area. At the other, on the far end of the country, after a Westerner blitzed the campus with Christian tracts, guards gave foreigners a close watch.

Walls seal off public parks, government compounds, companies and some private homes from the outside world. Families who have no room for a wall, pin posters of "door gods" by the entryway. Temples, too, station giant-sized idols like bouncers from hell on both sides of outside entrances.

For Chinese, "outside" and "inside" are just not the same.

Bill Holms suggested the word "Barbarian" captures the true emotional content of *waiguoren* better than "foreigner." There's also something to be said for "alien," which appears on Chinese customs forms. In remote villages, people have looked at me as if I'd stepped off a space ship. Children have run away or cried.

But however alien we may look to one another on occasion, China's contradictory feelings about walls are unfamiliar to none of us.

Why Build Walls?

In one of his witty essays, Holms complained about China's walls. To start with, the Great Wall:

"Is not worth seeing. . . It was. . . built by a mad paranoiac emperor who feared everything and whose passion was to box and freeze the world."

As for the other walls,

"The walls are only metaphors for the invisible walls between the Chinese and between China and the world. Power loves walls: people ought to hate them and tear them down."[3]

Holms echoed a feeling most visitors to China experience at some time. Are all foreigners really enemies? Do outsiders really have nothing more to share besides money or AIDS? Did the missionaries really come to China to make medicine from the eyes of Chinese children?

China can't lock itself inside the Wall forever. A country, like a pool of water, needs fresh input or it grows stagnant.

An individual can cut himself off from others in the same way.

I met a teacher in central China who, twenty years after the horrors of the Cultural Revolution took her husband, was still shy about leaving her apartment. She was a Christian, but was afraid to go to church. Her hands shook as she talked with me.

The walls of China are, contrary to Holms, an expression of something human and understandable. They are proof that while romantic dreamers tell themselves human beings can be trusted, a lot of painful experience teaches otherwise. In a "peach garden beyond the world" you might build a house or a city without protection. But in rural China or urban America, walls, locks, chains, guard dogs—even guardian spirits— are precautions few do without.

"In" is not the same as "out." Even poets and philosophers remember this when the sun goes down.

I arrived in the small Shandong coastal city of Weihai one evening after eight and began looking for a hotel. By nine, I found myself at the front desk of an establishment. But the receptionist took one look at my long white nose and showed me the door.

I refused to go. "My money is the same as anyone else's," I argued. After an hour's verbal combat she allowed that if I did stay, I'd have to reserve an entire room, unlike the Chinese who could take a single bed. "It's for your safety," her co-worker explained patiently. The fact it would cost me eight times as much as the Chinese had nothing to do with it. Besides, they weren't going to take me anyhow.

I was confident patience and desperation would pay off. They always had before. Anyway, I had nowhere else to go. I staked out a couch in the foyer and swatted mosquitoes.

But here the staff was made of stern stuff. My seige dragged on for three hours.

At midnight the security guard found sudden inspiration. He ran across the street to a run-down hostel not twenty yards from the front door. He came back excited. Yes, they would take a foreigner for the night.

The next day I heard about three Chinese from Manchuria. Apparently they'd also been unable to find an affordable room. They camped out in a public park—the only one nearby, I think. That night, the night the hotel staff tried to throw me out on the streets "for my protection," robbers stole their money and murdered them.

What do walls represent? From the inside, safety, friendship, home. From the outside, danger, mystery, and wonder. A wall is a border between two worlds.

What do doors signify? A passageway between worlds. "Here, and only here, may you enter. Come in if you belong. Come in if you are one of the family."

"Tom Opened The Door And Saw A Dragon"

Westerners too feel the difference between "in" and "out" as soon as we feel anything.

A door is a mystery children can't pass up. This morning my ten-month-old son climbed over me about twenty times in his effort to reach his holy grail of the kitchen floor.

G. K. Chesterton once wrote that for a child of eight it is exciting to hear: "Tom opened the door and saw a dragon," but for a child of three, it's enough to hear "Tom opened the door." A dragon is a symbol—of dogs, of rats, of death. The dragon's treasure is also a symbol—if only of strawberries and sugar.

I never believed in dragons or bogeymen as much as in the German Shepherd on the next block or the drunk at the end of the alley. Still the hairs on the back of my neck stood on end as I raced by the trap door that led under the house.

The door to the garage held a promise as well as danger, like the door to Tolkien's Mt. Doom. The garage was enchanted. I'd seen fire spit from the mouth of a metallic monster saw as it spit out chips and smoke, chewing through a two-by-four like the bones of a knight. Tools were piled like swords and suits of armor. Cans of magic water were buried under those piles that'd turn walls all the colors of the rainbow. If you pressed a certain button in one wall, the location of which the learned knew, one wall would swing open by itself! To me at that age, it was magic.

When I grew older the words "in" and "out" lost none of their magic. The wrong joke, the wrong haircut, and most of all the wrong friends, could mean the loss of acceptance. No one wants to be "out."

With each new door entered, a young person gains a new world, or rather a new part of the world becomes his. But he may also begin to sense that the door he really wants to enter swings in a different direction. Getting accepted, learning a new language, gaining skills, meeting people—fill stomach, mind, and hours. But none quite fill his soul.

The Drama Of The Door

Modern film mines the shallow end of the "door myth," rarely digging in its depths—usually bringing out more of its terror than its promise.

What will you find if you open your hotel door? A Mafiosi with a gun? Your wife with another man? A man-eating creature from outer space? Each genre of film relies on a different unhappy answer to the same set question. Recently the movie *Backdraft* provided a new fear: a ball of flame might surge through the opening and fry you. True, a spy may find a beautiful woman on his bed. But she, too, is dangerous.

The Greeks told of a woman named Pandora who was given a box and told not to open it. In the end, as echoed in a thousand horror stories since, Pandora opened her box, and plagues were released upon the world.

135

The Ark of the Covenant in Israel contained danger, too, but also hope. Steven Spielburg exploited its danger in *Raiders of the Lost Ark*. The climax of his film was the moment the Nazis pulled the lid of the arc and death rained on them. But Spielburg depicted this death with ghosts and evil spirits; he did not consider there might be something too beautiful and holy for us to view.

Why do they always open the door? Don't they know the director has put a monster or mobster behind it?

But there is no story, and thus no happy ending, if we leave doors closed.

What if, instead of something evil, we find ourselves face-to-face with God? What if in His eyes we see a reflection of something monstrous in our souls?

Or what if the box is empty?

Any religion, to be real to what is human, must provide an answer to the drama of the door.

The Wisdom Of Choosing

Buddha, like the Last Emperor of China, was born inside the walls of a palace. He spent his life trying to "escape." The freedom he found lay in making walls disappear. From the point of view of Zen, even the idea of "inside" and "outside" are without meaning.

Walls meant something to most Chinese, though. Even Buddhist monks built walls, and stationed gods and statues of monsters with big wooden eyes and ears to guard their gates. This shows that he who shuts himself out of a culture's common sense, will be taken in by its superstitions.

Marx fell into the same trap. He began by saying all peoples of the world should unite. His disciples ended up bolting China's doors tight, raising walls twice as high as before and throwing people who spoke English or French off fifth-floor balconies. Mao led China to war with most of her neighbors: the Soviet Union, Korea, Tibet, India, Taiwan, Vietnam, and with U.N. troops in Korea.

Like Buddha, Marx denied the logic of a fallen world and the hard choices it forces on us. By denying its logic both were fated to be swept away by its most illogical elements, by gullible rejection and gullible acceptance.

The Chinese have always known inside isn't outside. Strangers and family are two different things. Homeland is not the same as overseas. Heaven and earth are not equal. The two sides of a door look different, whether the door of a prison or of a palace.

Wisdom doesn't lie in opening doors. Nor does it lie in shutting them. Wisdom lies in knowing when to open and when to shut, whom

136

to let in and who to keep out. It lies in knowing when to stay put and when to look for another hotel.

This is the puzzle China has never been able to solve to its own satisfaction. Nor have foreigners helped. Whether they came to conquer, teach, or make money, each and every one has called on China to "tear down your walls." Each and every one has in the end given Chinese brick-makers a renewed sense of mission.

But one "foreigner" came to China not to tear down walls, but to open doors. He had with him a master key to let him in to peoples' hearts. It opens doors that have long been closed, doors creaking on their hinges and stiff with vines grown over centuries. This key lets China into the Truth it long sought.

Three gates symbolize the path Jesus took into the heart of China. The first is Tiananmen. The second is the gate at the Temple of Heaven. The third guards the tomb of Qin Shi Huang.

"Tea Mountain Yao" carve gates like these in the eastern mountains of Guangxi Province. Inside is not the same as out.

一門天賜平安福

Looking through Tiananmen Gate
to the Monument to the People's Heros.

Chapter Twelve

"One Gate Gives Peace And Happiness" — Jesus At Tiananmen

"*'Tian-an-men,'*" the librarian may have thought as he looked down on the crowd settling in for his most triumphant speech. "Who needs to talk about Heaven anymore? Here blood flowed on the earth. Red Square is what I'd rename this place, if the Russians hadn't beat me to it. Hmmmn." His eyes were drawn to the rear of the vast throng, to a more open space in the middle of the square. "This is what I'll do! I'll build a monument right there to the brave young people who died to bring me—us, all of China—through this gate. I'll call it the hero's monument—a monument to the people's heros."

The year was 1949, and Mao was standing on China's most famous door—Tiananmen, the hinge around which Chinese history has turned for four hundred years. Before him a vast field of cobblestone was filling with people, many soldiers who'd followed him into battle. The blood of both heros and villains had flowed to bring him there, first in the massacre of 1919 on this spot, then in hundreds of rice fields and forests and factories across China, and over ten thousand *li* of the Long March.

China had stood up. The gate was open. The people could stroll into the Forbidden City as emperors of the New China.

Mao himself, meanwhile, set up shop just to the west, in a parallel Forbidden City, and shut the gate.

Two decades later, Mao announced a "cultural revolution" from the same podium. Twenty more years, and students were gunned down in the square by those Mao had purged in the Cultural Revolution.

****

Why do rulers build walls? Why do subjects try to tear them down? What is the *Tao* of revolution, the principle that has kept China in a boil for thousands of years? How does shed blood renew the hope of a trampled and hopeless people? What is the meaning of this standing wave of living history called "Heaven Peace Gate" where rulers and ruled still face one another in hostile mistrust?

Is there really a gate through which one can pass into the Peace of Heaven?

China's "town square" is rich in meaning even deeper than the earth-shaking political events its stones have witnessed. The vast area of Beijing from the north end of the Forbidden City to the south end of Tiananmen Square, the heart of modern China, is an allegory in stone. It is a monument to the meaning of walls, to the hope of gates, to the pain of self-sacrifice, and to a love that can overcome even a tyrant's lust for power. Tiananmen means more than the path to political power: it is a symbol of the gate to spiritual peace.

Tiananmen was the front gate of he who called himself by the name of God. It is a metaphor of what it means to come home to God, and of the hero who laid his life down before the gate to let us in.

Why The City Was Forbidden

Yong Le, the son of the founder of the Ming Dynasty, first built the complex that Westerners (and, occasionally, Chinese) call the Forbidden

140

City about eighty years before Columbus sailed. Its more usual Chinese name is *Gu Gong*, the "ancient palace." A million workers carved stone and hauled timber for fourteen years to finish it. But within weeks, it burnt to the ground and had to be rebuilt.

The "Dragon Emperor" reigned behind three gates, each about 70 feet thick, the outer two separated by half a kilometer. One approached the dragon a bit winded, very intimidated, and fully aware of his power over common citizens. It's not hard to see why *Gu Gong* came to be called "forbidden."

What does the word "forbid" mean?

In Chinese the character is formed by joining two trees (林) and a promise. (示) - - - 禁

The Biblical story of the Garden of Eden also involves two trees and a promise. One was called the "tree of knowledge of good and evil." God told the first man and woman, "Do not eat of this tree, or you will die."[1] It was because of disobedience to this command that mankind was thrust from paradise. Angels guarded its front gate and "forbade" mankind access to the second tree, the "tree of life."

The Bible is the story of how the first implicit promise slowly became explicit: that one day the door would open again.

The emperor's palace was as remote from the average Beijing resident as the Garden of Eden. The state didn't employ angels to keep undesirables out, but eunuchs: men whose masculinity had been taken from them or which they gave up for a chance at high office. Japanese author Taisuke Mitamura explained their function:

"Neither God nor the monarch was to reveal what he actually was to the people—the secret door between the two worlds was always shut. But the monarch was only a man, so he led his private life behind doors in mysterious ways. He could not allow a commoner to enter his private quarters even as a servant, for that would mean disclosing himself to his people as a mere man, and he would have lost his control over the people."[2]

Eunuchs were a breed apart. Except for businessmen, who appreciated their free-spending ways, most people despised their effeminacy and eccentricity.

If other men must be allowed in, the rulers figured, first cut their ties to those outside by severing their sexuality. Not only did such creatures depend on their lord, they were physically unable to spawn rivals.

Such logic hasn't died out entirely. In Hong Kong, ninety-nine percent of the inhabitants are Chinese. But Filipino maids whom rich

Chinese hire to take care of their children fill Hong Kong's parks on their days off. Meanwhile, Sikhs from the Punjab in India have kept Hong Kong gates for generations.

A walk through Tiananmen towards the Forbidden City still takes one's breath away. Precipices of closely-laid rock tower on three sides to embrace or swallow visitors. The stone seems to whisper, "Behind us waits a dragon. Come in if you dare."

You could say Mao Tse Tung's promise to bring all China in was fulfilled. The gate is now open; visiting hours are posted, and everyone is free to walk in under a portrait of the Chairman which hangs over the central entrance.

But in another sense, too, Mao brought China into the throne room. He gave families across China a taste of palace intrigue. He taught China's "Old Hundred Names," as the masses of common people are called, fear and insecurity the emperor alone once knew. As Jesus warned, under Mao's regime it became brother against brother, and the members of families were often one another's enemies. Even today a foreigner, like a eunuch, can sometimes be allowed "in" precisely because he is so far "out." Total strangers have told me what they thought of communism, one adding, "I'd never tell this to another Chinese."

Noses At The Top Of The Wall

Tiananmen Square faces the emperor's front door across the street of Eternal Peace. Crowds of tourists on the square must look like ants from the top of that gate. The roads leading in have been engineered to shed water, making it look from ground level like the earth curves from one side of the street to the other. Government buildings rise like granite cliffs on three sides, only without pine tree or bird nest to break their sterility. In summer, pavement radiates heat, feet drag and minds glaze. Pedestrians feel alone, exposed, and small.

The dragon's front porch is big enough to swallow crowds. How often it has swallowed them!

The only structure that breaks up this flat expanse is a "Monument to the Peoples' Heros" which Mao built. He raised it to remember China's first student demonstrators to be killed, on May 4, 1919. That massacre set in motion the birth of the Communist Party. Four times since, Tiananmen has watched as China was transformed here—in 1949, 1966, 1976 and 1989. Here where sky meets earth, empires were born and died.

Tiananmen: Gateway To Power

As ancient Chinese saw it, the Emperor was "Son of Heaven," the ruler of earth who represented the human race before Heaven. How well he did this job went far to deciding the prosperity of the nation. Heaven might show its unhappiness in him by sending earthquakes, floods or famine. If he lost God's support, in the communist phrase, "rebellion was justified." Misrule might be so blatant the people rose against him almost by consensus.

There was one catch, though. If you took up arms against an emperor and won, you were vindicated. But if you lost, your sons might be hung in your presence, then you yourself slowly cut in pieces. This was the fate of assassin Chen De during the Qing Dynasty.[3] After a failed coup against Mao, Lin Biao tried to fly to the Soviet Union, but his plane ran out of gas and he crashed. Even if you got away, you would be cursed as both traitor and fool for misreading the will of Heaven.

And China would go on waiting.

The students in 1989 set up their "goddess of democracy" in the "central square" of the "central kingdom." The statue, as one journalist pointed out, was staring Mao's portrait of the entrance in the eye.

Tiananmen is like a slide projector. Place your image here, and it is magnified. One portrait of Mao over Tiananmen is worth a million on other walls. And its meaning is clear: "Power belongs to the people thanks to the Great Helmsman." The meaning of the "goddess" was equally clear: "We're grateful. Now it's time to let more of that power pass into the peoples' hands."

Tiananmen is a symbol both of how China knows people with power ought to act, and how China has seen them act. "Power corrupts." Here is power. Here, because power is wielded in pride, people who long for compassion and integrity from above have died.

Help Wanted: A True Son Of Heaven

Confucius advised rulers to win subjects over through respect.

"Rule over them with dignity and they will be reverent; treat them with kindness and they will do their best; raise the good and instruct those who are backward and they will be imbued with enthusiasm."[4]

Mo Zi added,

"One who obeys the will of Heaven will practice universal love.
. . the cunning will not deceive the simple, the noble will not
disdain the humble, the rich will not mock the poor, and the
young will not encroach upon the old. And the states in the
empire will not harass each other."[5]

Yet just when the wise advice these men and their disciples gave
China reached a peak of popularity, Qin Shi Huang united the nation
in blood.

Few of his successors flung away lives with quite his reckless
abandon. But "Sons of Heaven" continued to castrate poor men to
provide docile doormen. They stashed thousands of girls in their palaces
to meet every whim, even Hung pills. Many ministers, down to the
village level, followed this example as best they could afford. So did
Mao Tse Tung.

The Forbidden City was not just a barrier to the people. It was also
a trap for the emperor.

The movie *Last Emperor* portrayed Emperor Pu Yi as a child locked
in a huge closet. His eunuch "servants" were like a Machiavellian Island
of unwanted toys. He was locked in with them, and the world was
locked out. The contrast between imperial pretension and a child held
hostage in a play pen built for dragons created the moving pathos of
the film.

A World Outside

Could none of us identify? It's been said "No man is an island."
Often it seems as if we are all islands, and the water between us is filled
with sharks.

America, the "beautiful country," the goal of immigrants for a
hundred and fifty years, blessed with riches and land, must be one of
the most unhappy places in the world. Half of all marriages end in
divorce. Young people fill empty hours with pills, powders, and songs
about murdering police officers. Petty hatreds inflame rich
neighborhoods over a tree wrongly placed, a foot of land to the right
or left of a surveyor's mark, or a dog who poops on the wrong tuft
of grass.

Many who worked together in China during the Cultural
Revolution still hate each other. A woman who betrayed you, who
beat your father or sister until their faces bled, works in the same office
with you. Hour after hour, year after year, you turn around and there
she is. Nor does she say, *I'm sorry*. Nor does she expect to ever hear *I
forgive you*.

Why apologize? *It was Mao's fault. It was my boss' fault. Everyone was doing it.*

Why forgive? *She deserves whatever happens to her.*

The ancient realist Xun Zu took a hard look at society and wrote,

"Man is born, first, with a desire for gain. . . Second, man is born with envy and hate. . . Third, man is born with passions. . ."[6]

A Chinese proverb says "The heart of man is like a poisonous snake." It is easy for us to see his fangs when we look at our rulers, people of other political parties, our neighbors, or watch the daily news. It is harder to make out the dragon within.

A Western psychologist once wrote a book called *Denial of Death*, talking about the lengths to which people go to pretend they will live forever. We also take up a lot of energy in the "denial of sin."

Yet, the times in my life when I have learned the most have often been times of contending with the evil in my own heart. I remember how C. S. Lewis' words about pride in *Mere Christianity* showed me my own selfishness and arrogance. It was not a pleasant experience, but it was good for me. Likewise, one benefit of the Cultural Revolution is it left many in China willing to honestly reckon with human self-centeredness.

We find ourselves outside God's "ancient palace." Sin is the wall that keeps us from coming in.

We were the ones who left. "All we like sheep have gone astray," as the prophet Isaiah wrote, "we have turned every one to his own way."[7] But often we turn blindly, like dogs chasing their tales, for as Confucius noted: "When a man sins against Heaven he has nowhere to turn."[8]

The ancient Chinese acknowledged "Heaven loves the people"[9] and "He (Heaven) ascends and descends about our doings."[10] Yet they also felt, as Tsu Ch'an wrote, "The Way of Heaven is distant . . .what means have we of knowing it?"[11]

Is God our loving parent? Or distant and alienated? Both formulas fit many facts. Jesus, in his story of the son who left home and spent his Father's money in a "distant country," showed how both are true. God does love us. But we are outside the wall. We are lost in the slums of despair, wanting to come home but fearing the consequences of God's rule. We need to find a gate by which rebels and lost children are allowed into the king's palace.

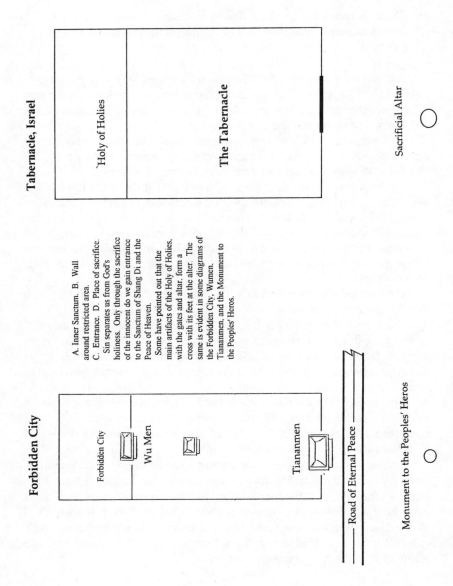

Tabernacle, Israel

Holy of Holies

The Tabernacle

Sacrificial Altar

A. Inner Sanctum. B. Wall around restricted area. C. Entrance. D. Place of sacrifice. Sin separates us from God's holiness. Only through the sacrifice of the innocent do we gain entrance to the Sanctum of Shang Di and the Peace of Heaven.

Some have pointed out that the main artifacts of the Holy of Holies, with the gates and altar, form a cross with its feet at the alter. The same is evident in some diagrams of the Forbidden City, Wumen, Tiananmen, and the Monument to the Peoples' Heros.

Forbidden City

Forbidden City

Wu Men

Tiananmen

Road of Eternal Peace

Monument to the Peoples' Heros

146

He has not forgotten us. His generous edicts are draped from the trees in spring. His laws whisper in our consciences. His proclamation of amnesty echoes distantly in the mythology of every culture.

But God did more than send messages. He sent His Son, the True Son of Heaven. Jesus walked out of the "ancient palace." He set down in the dirtiest, noisiest, roughest slum in town. He came to tell us about a gate through which we can gain entry to paradise again. He himself was that door, God's Tian-an-men.

Tian, The Son Of Heaven

The first character in Tiananmen is *Tian*, "Heaven."

Isaiah wrote of the coming savior as "Wonderful Counselor Almighty God." I can't think of another person, not Confucius, Paul, Mother Theresa, or Mahatma Gandhi, to whom such a title would stick.

The Son of Heaven didn't come with sword and cannon to storm the Forbidden City of our hearts. He came on foot, unarmed. The watchmen at the gate are free to let him in or shut him out. But there was no shyness in his knock. He came to restore the rule of Heaven.

An: Peace For Drug Addicts And Prostitutes

"*An*," the second character in Tiananmen, means "peace." The Bible calls Jesus the "Prince of Peace."

The Western plain of Taiwan is one of the most crowded and industrialized pieces of land in the world. But on the other side of a range of thirteen-thousand foot mountains lies paradise—blotted, as we have seen, by sin.

The Agape House Fellowship in Taiwan is a shaded quadrangle of buildings in the center of the strip of papayas and sugar cane, between the ocean and the hills. Frank and Annie, the American and Chinese couple who run the place, have a lot to do besides sheltering stress victims from the big city, but they were always hospitable when I dropped in. About fifty men and women were quitting methadone or amphetamines on my last visit. There were girls from nearby villages who'd been rescued from forced prostitution, too. A number of dogs made the center a refuge too, though the baboon that once sat in one of the trees had died. Troubled men and women seemed to like caring for animals.

Frank and Annie, who both have strong personalities, are good examples of how the rule of Jesus brings peace. The couple met during the Vietnam War. Frank, a young GI, dabbled in drugs in Vietnam. Later he transferred to Taiwan, where he met Annie at a party. The two set up a profitable business selling drugs. After marriage and a year or two of wheeling and dealing in Thailand, they moved to the States. There they kept up both with mind-altering chemicals and a serious interest in the occult.

Before long the drugs began causing problems. Doctors told Annie she was unable to bare children. Under stress from several directions, Frank and Annie's marriage began to unravel.

A Filipino doctor brought the couple to church. Christians prayed for Annie and prophesied she would give birth some day. Frank believed in Jesus that night and began reading the Bible voraciously. At first this irritated his wife. But, she told me later, one afternoon when she was worshipping Buddha, God spoke to her in a way which left her no doubt that He was alive and she would only find peace through Jesus.

The lives of this couple began to show in different ways how Jesus brings peace. First, he brought them spiritual peace. Second, by helping them love each other, He reconciled not only two individuals and two families but two very different cultures. He also brought peace to their bodies, not only freeing them from craving for drugs, but healing Annie's womb. Later she gave birth to a son they named Samuel.

Frank and Annie felt a desire to spread the peace they had found. They preached repentance and salvation in San Francisco's gay district—just before AIDS broke out among those who didn't listen. Later, they helped found an underground church in Saudi Arabia. After several years, they returned to Taiwan and began inviting drug addicts into their apartment.

Can prayer to Jesus bring peace to people with chemical dependencies? A report by Hong Kong University showed that a Christian drug center there was ten times as effective as the largest government-run center. I've met people from several Christian drug centers in Asia, including Frank and Annie's, and have mental pictures to go with the statistics. I know one-time heroin addicts, gangsters and pimps who've joined God's "peace process" in Asia.

I also visited a Christian half-way house near an American base in the Philippines where every year a hundred girls were rescued from prostitution and learned to help others.

People warped by every engine of destruction society can wield have found peace at the hands of Jesus: Opium addicts in Henan. Peasants in Sichuan. Professors in Shanghai. Headhunters in the mountains of Yunnan. Cut-throats in Burma. Slave-traders. Racists. North Ireland terrorists. People who've been at each other's throats for centuries. Not to mention millions of "ordinary" sinners like myself.

The "Prince of Peace." Who does that describe better than Jesus?

Men, **The Only Door**

"*Men*" (門) means door or gate. Jesus said,

"I tell you the truth, I am the door for the sheep. All of those who came before me were thieves and robbers, but the sheep did not listen to them. I am the gate; if any person enters through me he will be saved, and he will come in and out, and find pasture. The thief only comes to steal and kill and destroy; I have come so they have life, and have it more abundantly."[12]

The students who gathered in Beijing during the spring of 1989 may have been naive, but there is no denying their good will. They cared about China. Many died for the dream of a China free of tyranny, where rulers and ruled are at peace and authority holds hands with justice.

Normally, Sons of Heaven kill others to retain their power. But Jesus laid his own life down to gain for all people the "power to become the sons of God."

The Temple of Heaven, three miles south of Tiananmen, shows more of what it means to come in (來) to God's family.

Chapter Thirteen

Jesus At The Temple Of Heaven

It was a cold winter day in Beijing, and a brisk Siberian wind blasted dust down the empty streets of the capital. A finely-dressed but quiet procession issued from Tiananmen Gate: chariots drawn by shivering horses and elephants, musicians who didn't dare shiver. The emperor himself passed in silence. No street urchins called out at the parade.

It was winter solstice, four days before the Western Christmas. The Dragon Prince was going to the Temple of Heaven to pray to God.

"No more picturesque or impressive ceremony is to be found anywhere in the whole field of religion than the yearly sacrifice to Heaven," Charles Braden wrote in *The World's Religions*.[1]

Nor is it easy to find any more mysterious. Even Confucius admitted to being puzzled over this ancient annual ritual, which began long before his birth.

Perhaps Jesus had Confucius partly in mind when he told his followers: "Many prophets and kings desired to see the things you see and did not see them." For one secret those who witnessed the life and death of Jesus saw revealed was the ultimate meaning of the Temple of Heaven and the sacrifices held there.

Join the Emperor at prayer. Look up at the roof and pillars. Listen to the bleat of goats and the lowing of sacrificial cattle. Then open the Bible. Here the mystery of the temple, the greatest mystery of all, is solved—what it means for mortals to come into the house of God.

Meeting God In A Garden

The park where the emperor came is twice as large as already-enormous Tiananmen Square. Softened by cedars and cool green grass, despite its size it seems cozier and more pleasant. In the morning, when dew hangs from bent blades of grass, elderly residents of the capital sling cages with song birds from the cedars and stretch for *tai chi* exercises. Young Chinese play badminton and practice fencing. About where sacrificial animals were once put to death, instructors lead women in aerobics.

All other estates the emperor entered from the north. But in deference to Heaven, here he came in through the south entrance, the long way around. After his long walk he cautiously approached the building of which the "sun in its course" sees only one "so sublime."

Built on a marble terrace three levels above the surrounding ground, with nothing on the flat Beijing horizon to obstruct the view in any direction, the sky is bigger at the Temple of Heaven (*Tian Tan*) than in the rest of the park. Though *Tian Tan* only rises a few meters above the top boughs of the cedars, when you approach you feel like you're coming to the top of a mountain. It could be Mt. Tai, judging by its shape.

In the Forbidden City, it's hard to get rid of a suspicion the emperor might be lurking behind some wall with an army. But the Temple of Heaven, though more awesome in its quiet way, also seems more welcoming. God doesn't shout in this temple. But come early, avoid the tour groups, and you may hear His "still, small voice."

The Emperor came not just to hear from, but to speak to God. It would have been interesting to ask him: "Do you think God will come? Does the Creator of the galaxies really hold conferences with his earthly chieftains at the winter equinox?" And then, if your head still remained on your shoulders: "Can you empathize now with underlings who petition you? Did you sleep last night?"

Jesus At The Temple Of Heaven

The Chinese weren't copying foreign symbolism when they built this structure, as we saw in the first chapter. The temple was built to restore true Chinese religion.

Yet in many ways, that edifice points to Jewish religious experience and the climatic episodes in the life of Jesus.

First, the Temple of Heaven reminds us that the Chinese, like the Jews, worshiped a holy God: a God who cared about man, who, unlike other Chinese gods, should not be represented by idols.

What you notice as you approach the building is its three-level blue-tile roof. The color scheme may have been an accidental result of fire damage. The original temple had a multi-colored roof; after a fire, the architects bought just blue tiles, perhaps to economize. But from a Christian perspective, what better way to represent the God of heaven, who is three persons in one?

The Temple of Heaven also reminds us the Chinese did not feel a visit with God was a light matter. Why else did the man called "Son of Heaven" come only once a year? Why else was his visit an occasion for cautious ceremony and justifiable trembling? The nation knew that emperors, too, were subject to the judgement of Heaven.

By definition, for a creature to meet its Creator would transcend all other experience. Yet Chinese and Jewish traditions suggest certain roles—as student, child, or citizen—can give us a hint of the emotions we may feel at this meeting.

Whether or not the emperor, while living, came especially close to Him whom we all meet after death is an open question. But many people have. We can also learn from their experiences. Finally, as we look closer at the architecture of Tian Tan, and at the Chinese language, we find hints of what can be done so that the meeting will be a joyful one.

"Awesome Heaven God Above" plaque at Temple of Heaven.

The Test

So much of the hopes of a Chinese scholar have always rested on how he did on exams. The pressure he felt was compounded by the fact that his family's hopes, too, often rode on his success. Some found it too much: one failed student in the 19th Century went crazy and started China's bloodiest revolution, the Taiping Rebellion.

But once there was a dreamy young student named Wang Zhen Xiao. As Wang read and reread the Confucian classics which would be the basis of the exams, his thoughts suddenly took an unexpected and impractical turn. "Was this written only to help me snag a government job?" The question came to him. "Wasn't it really written to make me a better person?" And so he "set his heart on Way." He took time from study to teach his sisters. He took a crippled villager under his wing and taught him landscape painting. He began to spend less time with books and more with poverty-stricken neighbors than some thought prudent.

Wang felt Confucius was a hard act to follow. He was frustrated by an inability to hold his temper. Also, as the day of the exam drew near, he began to think more of what his parents would do if he failed. Confucius' disciples might have made do with an elbow for a pillow; but in his family better things were hoped for.

One night the young student fell into a feverish dream. He saw himself sitting in a spacious room, accompanied by an old man in the road-worn vestment of an earlier dynasty. The man looked him in the eye. "This is your test," he said. "There is a cubicle on your right. In it, you will find the one you both fear and hope to meet. Tell him what you have done with your life."

Imagine you were he. You are about to meet the person on whose teachings or example you have leaned all your life. If you are a Red Guard, it might be Chairman Mao. If you are a photographer, perhaps you'll meet Ansel Adams, or one of the great nature painters of the Qing dynasty. If you are a social worker, it might be Mother Teresa waiting behind the door.

Here before you is one who sees what you see and cares about what concerns you. A pat on the back from this person would make you stand taller the rest of your life.

Is this not one way to anticipate what it might mean to meet God? One day, the Bible says, the Author of all the good that is in us will say to some, "Well done."

The Prodigal Princeling

Jesus said meeting God would also resemble the return of a runaway child to a loving Father. It is easy to re-cast the story he told in terms of recent Chinese history.

Doctor Lao Shi was one of that idealistic breed of cadres swept into power on the heels of the revolution. He would go hungry before charging a fee to an impoverished patient. He'd walk twenty miles before accepting a ride from a higher official that might be misconstrued. He was an asset to the Party and the nation.

But honesty is not always a personal asset, and during the Cultural Revolution, Dr. Shi was dragged before a kangaroo court and sent to prison.

His son, Shi Bu Dong, disowned his father and left home.

Bu Dong was caught up in the political madness of the day. Every day seemed a blur of struggle, shouting, and parades. It seemed easier that way. But then his gang split in three factions and he was caught up in bitter and bloody personal feuds. Then he and his friends were "sent down" to a remote farming district in the hills, and he had time to reflect.

At night, the moon seemed to stare at him with his father's sad eyes. "I gave you life." It seemed to say. "I taught you the way to go. Why did you betray me?"

Several years passed. Bu Dong received a letter.

"Dear Bu Dong," it read. "I have been rehabilitated. Come home." It was signed by his father.

The next morning, having caught the first bus, he stood outside the door of his father's home. His legs felt like noodles. He half hoped the ground would swallow him. But he also began to feel cleansing in a heart that had grown tired of hatred. He had never been able to cast the image of his father from his mind, and he longed to see him again.

Bu Dong opened the door, and heard his father's strong voice: "Come in, son!"

Jesus said angels rejoice at the repentance of one who comes home to God. But his story of the Prodigal Son also shows that a gate exited in eager haste, is often re-entered only after much soul-searching.

****

When a minister from the provinces walked through Tiananmen Gate, it was likely neither awe nor shame that made his legs go weak, so much as simple, animal fear. Whether or not the present ruler inspired respect, and whether or not the present official was inclined to give it, one fact stared all those who entered the Ancient Palace in the face: "This man can have your life."

Unlike many in our age, Jesus seemed to feel this primitive emotion, a sense of danger in the presence of the transcendental, was healthy and reasonable. "Don't be afraid of those who kill the body," he warned disciples. "No, I'll tell you whom to fear: fear him who can not only kill, but cast into hell."[2]

****

The Temple of Heaven is now visited by thousands of tourists every day for whom it is only one more stop on a long itinerary. Every day we too drive or peddle or stroll by churches, mosques, and synagogues, with hardly a glance. You'd expect a house of worship, or private prayer, to excite a feeling of cosmic vulnerability, what the Bible calls "fear of the Lord." But sometimes about all we feel is boredom or aching knees. Maybe that's all the emperor felt. Perhaps he thought God was ignoring him. Maybe he preferred it that way. Maybe he even asked himself if *Huang Tian Shang Di* were more than illusion.

But once in a while, the door eases open a crack, and doubts are swept away in a whirlwind.

"Heaven Came Down And Glory Filled My Soul"

The Bible says in the beginning, man and God had fellowship, and there was no terror in that communion. But then Adam and Eve ate "forbidden fruit," and as soon as they heard holy footsteps, they ran and hid in the bushes.

Fear of God came through sin. But just as pain must precede healing, so now, none come close to God, unless they know a holy and healing terror first.

The door opened on Israel's teacher of the Way. The Bible says "Moses hid his face, for he was afraid to look at God." [3] The vision within dropped prophets to their knees: "Woe to me!" cried Isaiah, "I am ruined! For I am a man of unclean lips, and I live in the midst of a people of who have unclean lips, yet I have seen the king, the Lord Almighty.'"[4] It humbled patriarchs: "I had heard of you, but now I see you with my own eyes," said the "righteous man," Job. "Therefore I look at myself with contempt and repent in dust and ashes." [5]

Daniel gave perhaps the most personal and psychologically detailed account of such a moment:

"The men with me did not see the vision, but such a great terror fell on them that they ran off to hide. . . I had no strength left, the color drained from my face and my power was gone. . . I stood up trembling. Then he said to me,'Don't be afraid, Daniel'. . . I said to the one standing before me, 'I am filled with anguish because of the vision, my lord, and am without strength. How can I, your servant, talk with you, my lord? My strength is gone and I can't breathe." [6]

Modern experience has been very similar. In the year 1799 renewal swept across America. One eyewitness wrote how under the influence of God's Spirit five hundred or more people were swept to the ground "as if a battery of a thousand guns had been opened up." Francis MacNutt wrote that after a sermon by John Wesley in Bristol, England, some in the audience "cried as in the agonies of death," and fell to the ground, groaning.

During the 1930s similar scenes were witnessed in Shandong Province and other places in China. In one Christian school during a revival meeting a missionary watched a student, who'd help foment dissent as member of a communist cell group, fall on the ground. He called out, "Oh God! If you won't crush me to death, I will confess my sins." [8]

Yet when people yielded to their hearts to God, fear was swallowed in joy and wonder.

A missionary who was also tried by the fire of God's presence in the Shandong revival wrote,

> "For days and days to come I have never seen or heard of such conviction of sin. The Spirit was no respecter of persons; no missionary escaped, no leader or worker among the Chinese escaped; old and young alike, rich and poor, were the same. For three days after I had made my confession I just sat there in the meetings sometimes as long as eight and ten hours a day and praised the Lord for his mercies. My whole body seemed to be going through a great change. It seemed like a strong electric current was going through my body. . . Sometimes I felt like I would die for joy, at others I would be crushed under the burden of prayer." [8]

Charles Finney, a catalyst for revival in America during the 19th Century, witnessed many such scenes. Being a lawyer, he tried to analyze them. He said it was as if a veil were "removed from the mind," and people saw truth naked, as at the moment of death. He added, "No wonder this should overpower the body."[9]

It is possible to copy the effects this "outpouring" sometimes produces. Thus some think it is spiritual to fall down in prayer meetings,

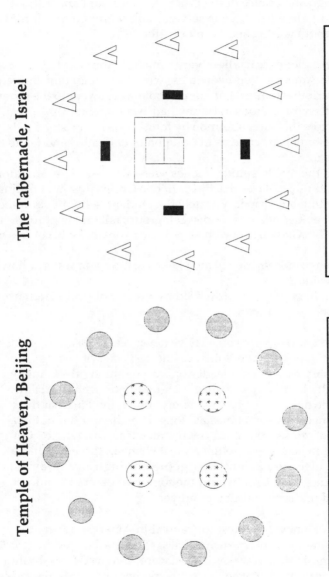

The Tabernacle, Israel

One man came once a year to pray and sacrifice to God for all the people. Twelve tribes were arranged in four groups around the tabernacle. Twelve pillars representing the tribes were set up in a special ceremony and the people were sprinkled with animal blood.

Temple of Heaven, Beijing

One man came once a year to pray and to sacrifice to God for all the people. Four gold and red pillars are surrounded by twelve red pillars on the outside. Animals were sacrificed outside.

or shout, or for everyone to pray out loud together. Even Maoist "self-criticism" may have aped (using fear and hatred rather than love for the fuel) external signs of the outpouring of God's Spirit. But the true signs of God's presence are a deep shame over personal sin, a sense of the holiness of God, and then joy nothing else can match at finding forgiveness in Christ.

I have known this joy on a personal level, a little. But only once, during a retreat in Taiwan, did I experience this kind of group revival. And then it was only like a few, heavy drops of rain from thunderclouds still waiting to burst.

A door locked for a lifetime swings open. Facing us is something that is to the spirit as the sun would be to the eyes if it were in the next room. It overloads our spiritual retinas. It shines through our souls like an x-ray. It exposes truths about ourselves which like cobwebs we had tried to ignore.

Chinese culture provides two remarkable pictures of how Jesus can turn the greatest fear into eternal joy. The Temple of Heaven is one.

In Israel, as in China, once a year one man approached the Temple. Like the emperor, the day the Jewish high priest came to meet God was filled with suspense, for he too came to pay the bill for a nation's sins. As in Beijing, he offered livestock—cattle, sheep, goats.

But if God is a sun in the next room, the death of animals or a ceremony by a ruler cannot shield us any more than a silk screen across a door. They are fine as symbols, but only provide an illusion of protection.

The room farthest from the outer gate, the Holy of Holies, was fenced off behind a line of chains, and guarded by fifteen-foot angels. This reminded the Jewish people that no man could peer into the presence of God and live.

Yet there are symbols of hope, too.

The Jewish temple was inlaid with gold, and engraved with figures of angels, palm trees and flowers. These ornaments reminded Israel of the Garden of Eden, where God first blessed. They also reminded worshipers that one day the gate to paradise would swing open again.

When you stand in the center of the Temple of Heaven, four gold and red pillars surround you on the inside. Twelve more red pillars rise on the outside. In the same way Moses positioned three tribes of Israel on four sides of the Tabernacle; twelve in all.

Why gold? A Chinese proverb says "Gold fears no fire." Gold retains its purity, like the Word of God. One who is pure has nothing to fear in the presence of God. Thus four pillars, as four Gospels tell of the only man who need not fear the fire of God's holiness. Covered with his righteousness, we too can stand pure.

Why red? Red represents redemption. In an ancient ceremony, Moses sprinkled blood onto the twelve tribes around him, and onto twelve pillars.

The death of animals was a symbol. But one day, another sacrifice would open the gate to Heaven. "Because of our sins he is wounded," wrote Isaiah, "we are healed by the punishment he suffered, made whole through his injuries." [10]

Red and gold pillars in the Temple of Heaven

The rulers were out for blood. One of Jesus' own disciples offered to betray him. When they saw which way the wind was blowing, the crowds swung against him too. Soldiers arrested the rabble-rouser in the middle of the night. They beat him and dragged him before the local party bosses.

The trial was over in a few hours. The verdict: "Guilty!" Guilty of impersonating God. Guilty of offering false hopes. Guilty of insulting the authorities.

The Bible calls Jesus the "Lamb of God" who "takes away the sin of the world."

Thus the twelve pillars, and the twelve around those, symbolizing God's kingdom among men, are red, as if covered with the blood of sacrifices.

義 is the Chinese character for "righteousness." On top is " 羊 " (yang), sheep or goat. This animal, used both in Jewish and Chinese temples, "covers" the character " 我 ," (Wo), "me." From above, all you see is the sheep. "When Heaven sees me covered by the lamb, I am righteous."

"Come"

One final, amazing picture of Jesus' sacrifice for us is found in the Chinese word " 來 " or "Come."

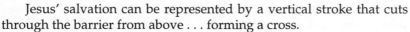

The first stroke in this character is a horizontal slash, ━━━ .

This represents the alienation we feel from God. We read the signs on faces in the streets around us: faces that speak of arguments, back-biting, betrayals, romance gone sour, friendships and families broken. Like the stone wall around the Forbidden City, a wall stands between us and paradise. We feel a painful gap between what we are and what we know we should be.

Jesus' salvation can be represented by a vertical stroke that cuts through the barrier from above . . . forming a cross.

What was a cross? It was a piece of wood to which a criminal was nailed until he died. In countries like Japan and Palestine, it was the cruelest measure the government could take against a criminal.

A "cross" is also a way from one side of a barrier to the other.

Put a man, 人 , on the cross, and what do you have? The Chinese character for "wood" or "tree" emerges.

The Bible says the man Jesus didn't die on the tree alone. Two criminals were hung beside him, "One on his right, the other on his left."[11]

Add these two figures to our picture.

"Person person," (人人), means "all people" in Chinese. It seems these two cutthroats were meant to represent all mankind. This arrangement may seem unreasonable to you. You take care of your family. You pay your taxes. Yet those who make the study of the psyche their profession, tell us dark things go on in the hearts of the decent and respectable people every day. God, looking deeper still, ordained that these two bandits represent the human race. "All have sinned, and fallen short of the glory of God," the Bible says.[12]

Also, like those two men, we will die. Hopefully it won't come so publicly or painfully. We may be sedated and surrounded by flowers and cards. But however it comes, what they faced, we will face some day.

What happened to those two men?

I once watched a man I think was a drug smuggler carted away in a pickup truck near China's southern border to be shot. He raised his hand to a friend in the crowd in a show of defiance or bravado, as if to show contempt for the sentence being carried out on him. There was no repentance in his action. The *Gospel of Luke* says one of these criminals made a similar motion. He mocked the "holy man" who hung next to him. "Are you really the Christ?" He sneered. Hatred lent him a second wind. "Then save yourself, and us too!"[13]

The other man looked in Jesus' eyes, and in that instant had an experience like the young man who met Confucius, or the prodigal who looked in the eyes of his father again, or the missionary in the Shantung revival. Instantly all earlier fears and hopes seemed foolish as awe overwhelmed him. He shouted at his comrade in amazement. "Don't you fear God? We're getting what we deserve."

In every revival even "holy people," missionaries, preachers and others who are dedicated to God's work, become aware that in the end they are just like that criminal—and sometimes, because of their hypocrisy, even worse. We, too, "Deserve our fate." Because of the man on the tree, though, we get something better.

The second thief saw this too. "But this man hasn't done anything wrong," he went on. Then he turned back to Jesus. "Remember me when you come into your kingdom," he asked simply.

Jesus answered—his final, shocking statement—"Today you will be with me in paradise."[14]

How strange, thought the mob. A dead man granting life! A criminal forgiving another criminal! The famous rabbi consorting with bad elements to the end! With Jesus' respectable enemies, the other bandit may have laughed a good, final laugh.

But the other man died in peace.

Add one human figure to Jesus' right, and one to his left, and the character "Come" is formed.

Jesus gave a simple answer to the bandit's simple request.

"Today you will be with me in paradise." You and I will *Come* in together. Into a garden of pomegranates. Into a city of crimson and gold. Into the presence of the Father.

"And when Jesus cried out again with a loud voice, he gave up his spirit. . . And suddenly the curtain of the emple was torn in two from top to bottom." [15]

Savior and saved both died.

At that moment, the veil between man and God was shredded "from top to bottom." The door was open. Salvation—as all cultures have always instinctively known—was beyond our grasp. But we—as every people has vaguely seen through myth and dream—were not beyond God's. That's what the Temple of Heaven was built to remind us. That's what the Chinese character "Come" proclaims. "The man on the cross bridges the gap between Heaven and earth and allows all who follow to Come in to God."

There is just one question left to answer. What did they see when they crossed the threshold of death?

"It is completed." Shatin, Hong Kong.

Funeral for a young teacher, Zhuang people, Guangxi. A heavy
drinker, he killed himself, leaving a wife and young son. Like
most tribal peoples, the mountain tribes of southern
China are plagued with alcoholism and other problems.

Chapter Fourteen

Door Into The Earth

Qin Shi Huang, the self-styled "Savior of China," was afraid. All
human foes had been defeated, but his Taoist advisors with their magic
mushrooms and herbs of the gods didn't seem able to do anything about
the enemy now facing him. "The first emperor hated any talk of dying,"
the historian tells us, "and none of his advisors dared allude to the
matter of death."[1]

Nevertheless, Emperor Qin did die, ironically on the border of
Shandong Province. His officials carted him home, but by the time his
procession arrived in the city of "Eternal Peace," it was too late. "His
presence was manifest through the olfactories," as one Victorian writer
tenderly put it.[2] To mask the smell, his ministers bought a large quantity
of fish.

For a man who didn't care to talk about death, Qin had done an
extraordinary job of planning for it. While his second son followed in
his father's bloody footsteps by murdering twenty-two siblings, the
old emperor was placed in a tomb such as Steven Spielberg never
pictured in his wildest dreams. The portion unearthed in the Twentieth
Century, with its terra-cotta warriors and horses, has become one of

the wonders of the ancient world. But that was only a small part of the total tomb complex.

Over thirty years, before many (it is said) were entombed alive for their troubles, Qin's 700,000 craftsmen and laborers (three times the number that worked on the largest Egyptian pyramid) did much more than make figurines. They dug through subterranean streams, sealing them off with bronze. They filled Qin's tomb with delicate pottery, precious stones, and rare odds and ends from around China. They built models of palaces, pavilions and other imperial buildings. Artisans drew on the best technology available to create models of the ocean and the rivers of China, making them flow and circulate with mercury. Pearls shone from the roof of this underground empire in the pattern of the stars, while gold and silver birds and jade pine trees brightened the floor. Crossbows were set to mechanically shoot intruders.

Finally, the historian Ssi Ma reports,

"Lamps were fueled with whale oil so that they might burn forever."[3]

You can't take it with you? Qin was going to try. If eternal happiness could be assured by a well-built tomb, the emperor would be the happiest man in the other world.

But to us, there seems to remain an element of pathos or even comedy in the project. There he lies: the mighty emperor, tucked like a frightened child under a blanket of sod, a clay cavalry of over-sized toy soldiers around his bed, with a night light left on to comfort him.

The soldiers did their job, though. For two thousand years, Qin's magnificent, yet horrifying nursery lay undisturbed. No one broke in.

On the other hand, no one broke out, either.

So in the end, death had the last laugh. As usual.

From the world's mightiest ruler to peasants so poor their wives pull the plow, most people understand Qin's fear. Before us waits a gate that is easy to enter, but hard to exit. Here is a door that fulfills the promises or threats made by every other. It really does open on another world.

But thank God, we have a guide through this door.

Dying Chinese Style: Does Goodbye Have To Mean Forever?

One of the most enduring Chinese hopes is that some sacrifice by the living can bridge the wall of immortality.

Chinese usually lay their departed to rest on hillsides. Often the spot that has the best *feng shui*, "wind water," or balance of natural elements intended to give peace to the dead, also has a beautiful view of hills and fields. A little strip of wood called an ancestor tablet is marked with the name and sometimes the date of death of the deceased. This tablet, which traditionally was thought to be one of the three resting places of the soul, is placed on the family altar and worshiped. During the *Qing Ming* festival in the spring, Chinese make a holiday by these hill-top resting spots, bringing choice delicacies which their ancestors especially liked.[4]

The people of Nagasaki, Japan, influenced by Chinese settlers, play an interesting variation on this theme. During the "Obon" festival, families troop up Nagasaki's ubiquitous hills to graves in the late afternoon. They line up oblong yellow lanterns by their ancestors' tombs and send bottle rockets whistling into the evening sky. If a family lost a member that year, they build a boat of bamboo and wood for him, covering it in cedar bows, plastic flowers, and paper lanterns. They hang a large photograph of the deceased on the bow. Then, scattering fireworks like rose petals at a wedding, they escort his spirit to the harbor. Having walked him out the first year, next year he'll find his own way back to the world of the dead, they hope.

Touring The Far Side Of Death

No mortal really finds *Qing Ming*, or *Obon*, or Halloween, or seances, that mystifying. The grave is the highest and most pitiless barrier, a big black Berlin Wall that sooner or later cuts us off from each other. Just as the Taiwan Straits separated families on the mainland and in Taiwan for forty years, so the river of death divides us. Who doesn't want to find some gap in this barrier? Old family albums aren't enough: we want a reunion. "Tear down the wall!" We cry. "Re-open relations!"

But the Bible says "Not so fast." Look before you leap. This wall, like all walls, protects only as long as it divides. This is why the author of Deuteronomy warned,"Don't let be found among you any who. . . is a medium or wizard or who talks with the dead," [5]

Why is the Christian God so strict? Why does He object to letting us "reach out and touch" those we love—if we can?

"Don't be so naive," say the Scriptures. If earthly walls hide tyrants and gangsters, why should we assume all is light and beauty in the spiritual realm? In fact, "like lions looking for prey" an enemy lurks in the shadows of eternity in wait for us.

Many laugh at talk of the devil. But here again, in their naivity, they are like frogs in a well.

Human sacrifice demanded by the gods is said to have been the single unifying factor among the pre-Christian tribes of Europe. It was also common among China's tribal peoples. Quacks and tyrants from Qin to Mao relied on the occult. So has nearly every charismatic lunatic

Escorting spirits of newly departed loved ones to the harbor. Does goodbye have to mean forever?

A Chinese grave.

Old stone gate and peach or plum blossoms. A ripe
peach symbolizes longevity. When we pass through
the gate of death will we find eternal life?

in the modern world who dropped cyanide in a vat of koolaid or gassed
a commuter train. I and close friends have met people who also blurred
the line that separates the living from the spirit world. The price they
paid was visible in their eyes. As I mentioned earlier, most were suicidal.

You don't have to study Christian theology to want to keep a
distance from the other side. Here again we need a "Middle Way"
between naive skepticism and blind belief.

God knows we hanker to rip a hole in the "Berlin Wall" of death.
In Jesus He provides a way to satisfy our deepest hungers—for hope,
life, even for a holiday—without dragging our souls "out on a limb"
into the dark fringes of necromancy. But the answer is not Halloween,
the season when things die. It is Easter, when things come to life.

The Knob Turns

The True Son of Heaven, having died, was placed in a tomb. A
boulder was rolled across the hole that marked its entrance. Under
orders from Pontius Pilate, the Roman official who agreed to his murder,
soldiers were stationed to guard the site. Unlike that guarding Emperor
Qin, this was no ceramic honor guard. Rumors had reached the ruler's
ears that disciples might steal their Master's body. The soldiers were
of flesh and blood, and well armed. They were there to keep Jesus in.

Two days later some women who followed Jesus decided, like Qin's
ministers, to try to mask the smell of their Master's mortality. They
brought spices to the tomb.

Visiting an ancestor, Obon festival, Nagasaki.

Like many before and since, these peasant women came with heavy
hearts. Jesus had told them, as he stumbled to the place he would die,
"Don't weep for me, weep for yourselves."[6] No doubt they did. Their
Master was gone; they were left behind. They had no strength to roll
the stone away from his grave. How much less would they be able to
push off the dirt that would, in a few "nasty, brutish and short" years,
cover their own?

His voice had sounded, as the proverb said, like a "fountain of
life." They'd heard him tell storms "Be calm"—and stillness prevailed.
They watched him exorcise evil spirits from the possessed and madmen
became sane. By his command the blind saw and the lame walked.

Now their hopes seemed cheated. They could not silence the jeering
last words of the thief on the cross. "You can't even save yourself!
What hope can you bring me?"

170

The Master of Life was dead. All joys, like the jewels of a dead king, seemed buried under earth with him. If the soldiers had a heart, they would push away the boulder in front of his tomb, and say goodbye to a good man who failed.

But at the tomb nothing was in its expected place. The soldiers were gone. The rock was off to one side. And Jesus—Where was Jesus?

"He is not here. He is risen."

So it was reported to the women, anyway. And then they saw him, and they passed the news on to his other followers.

Soon the disciples were preaching it in the market places. Then one of his enemies saw him too, and became his most fanatical follower —the Apostle Paul. Because this band of harried believers persuaded a skeptical public Jesus was alive, most of the world takes a break from work every Sunday. Because of that testimony, we have a Christian church, a Western civilization, a modern world.

The Only Mystery Is There Is No Mystery

In chapter nine I mentioned A. N. Wilson, the English biographer. Wilson, having read a wide spectrum of skeptical comment on the life of Jesus, wrote his own book. Like other skeptics, Wilson tried to "read between the lines" of the Gospels. Jesus' plans and motives, the hidden thoughts of his enemies—often when the narrative was silent, Wilson, like dozens of skeptical scholars over the last two hundred years, came up with a hypothesis.

I was surprised, with all his speculation, Wilson could not claim to know what happened Easter morning:

> "We have reached the point in our narrative where we must abandon our efforts to pursue 'what really happened.'"[7]

Kerry Temple, editor of *Notre Dame* magazine, wrote a long article tracing skeptical theories of the "historical" Jesus. In the end he made a similar admission.

> "The events following his crucifiction have become a veritable mystery. . . No one is certain precisely what it was that happened."[8]

That is like standing at the confluence of three rivers at flood stage and complaining of draught.

Mystery? There is no mystery. The evidence roars like flooding waters.

Wilson overheard a tour leader at Jesus' tomb referring to the resurrection as "The best-attested fact" in history. That man was right. There is a flood of evidence that Jesus did rise from the dead—far more evidence than for any other event in ancient history.

The testimony of several eyewitnesses and near-eyewitnesses, written within just a few years of the events, lies ready at hand.

Luke, an intimate of eyewitnesses, wrote, "While they were still talking about this, Jesus himself stood among them and said to them, 'Peace be upon you.' But they were terrified and frightened, thinking they'd seen a ghost. He said to them, 'Why are you upset, and why do doubts come up in your minds? Look at my hands and my feet. It is I myself! Touch me and see; a ghost doesn't have muscles and bones, as you see I have."[9]

John, Jesus' closest friend, wrote, "Then he said to Thomas, 'Put your finger here; and look at my hands. Stick your hand out and put it into my side. Don't doubt, but believe.'"[10]

Paul, writing twenty-five or so years after the events: "Christ died for our sins according to the Scripture, (he) was buried, and (he) rose again on the third day according to the Scriptures, and (he) was seen by Peter, and then to the Twelve. After that, he was seen by more than five hundred of the brothers at the same time, most of whom are alive to this moment, though some have fallen asleep. Then he was seen by James, then by all the apostles, and last of all he was seen by me also. "[11]

The account in the Gospel of Mark seems to be based on the testimony of two eyewitnesses: Peter and Mark himself.

Beginning three days after its founder's public execution, Christianity exploded on the ancient world. What fueled the new movement's amazing growth? The heart of every sermon the apostles preached was Jesus' death and resurrection. Nothing—not whips, crosses, or lions—could make them change their story.

Historian Thomas Arnold noted:

"I have been used for many years to study the histories of other times, and to examine and weigh the evidence of those who have written about them, and I know of no one fact in the history of mankind which is proved by better and fuller evidence of every sort."[12]

Often we Christians are accused of poking pins in other peoples' balloons. We frown on firecrackers and dragons, rail against ancestor worship, and shun parades of spirits.

Jesus didn't give in to easy sentimentalism when it came to dead loved ones, either. "Let the dead bury the dead," he said to a man who thought his father's funeral more urgent than his own salvation.

But neither skepticism nor witchcraft offer any real hope at the door of death—only despair, or indulgence.

Jesus died for our sins and came to life again. He calls us to follow him. That is the answer to the deepest need in every culture: a way through death into life.

****

Christianity is looking less and less like a foreign religion in today's China. Various observers debate whether the church has grown to twenty, fifty or seventy million. What no one denies is that the "Jesus teaching" has taken firm root in Chinese soil—becoming the most dynamic spiritual movement in China today, though most Chinese have yet to hear the Good News of Jesus.

Who is the medium for this message? I visited one town in southern China where only a scattering of Christians was reported to exist. A year or so later I came back, and there were several hundred. I met the evangelists from far across China who were responsible. They asked me to relay to the world outside, "Pray for us," mentioning persecution as one of their chief concerns.

In a nearby town I met a young man who had been cured of a severe injury through prayer, resulting in a small revival in his village. I met a university graduate who was teaching English and the Gospel to tribal young people. I also met a doctor who had recently become a Christian, who traveled to remote villages to heal the sick. "No other doctors come to those places," he told me, "So they're really glad to see me. They're very poor, and some have sold all their livestock to buy opium."

I've had the privilege of meeting many self-sacrificing, courageous Christians in China, who take great risks to bring great blessings: healing, casting out demons, preaching the good news of Jesus. If you want a full account of what they are doing and what is being done to them, especially in the central provinces, read the book of *Acts*.

Why did China wait so long to respond? Perhaps we Westerners got in the way. Maybe Marxism did China a favor by ripping the blinders of superstition off many. Certainly we should not forget the courage of those preachers.

But I am also reminded of Jesus' words, "I am the resurrection and the life. He who believes in me, even if he dies, he will live." I am inclined to think that, most of all, the Gospel needed to be buried, like Jesus, before it could rise again. I am inclined to think that when the best God offers is contemptuously stomped on, buried and forgotten in the ground, God likes to see it rise from the ground again. China has always awaited a spring that would touch not only the plants, but the hearts of men. Now it has begun in the Middle Kingdom.

Harvest time in China.

Notes

(All Biblical quotes are paraphrases.)

Chapter One

1. Archibald E. Glover A Thousand Miles of Miracle OMF Press
2. Bill Holm Coming Home Crazy Bill Holms Milkweed Editions, 1990
3. Su Shi Kang, Wang Lu Xiang He Can North City Jin Feng Publication Co. Ltd.
4. W. A. P. Martin Cycle of Cathay Edinburgh O. Anderson and Ferrier,1896.
5. Huston Smith Religions of Man New York Harper & Row, 1958. p.15

Chapter Two

1. Acts 17:23
2. Chen JingPan Confucius as a Teacher Beijing Foreign Language Press, p.97
3. The Pin-Yin Chinese-English dictionary Beijing Foreign Language Press,p.149
4. Frena Bloomfield The Book of Chinese Beliefs: A Journey Into the Chinese Inner World Arrow, 1983
5. Clifford Plopper Chinese Religion Seen Through the Proverb New York Paragon Book Reprint, 1969. p. 72
6. Ibid. p.76
7. Charles Braden The World's Religions p.142

8.Missing.

9. Zhong Guo Zhe Xue Zhu Yao Fan Chou Gai Nian Jian Shi Hangzhou, China: Zhejiang People's Press. p.206

10. Chen Jing Pan Confucius as a Teacher Beijing Foreign Language Press, p.100 quoting Book of Poetry 3,3,2

11. Ibid. p.99 (quoting Tao Chuan, under the 14th year of Duke Hsiang)

12. Ibid. p102 quoting Book of Poetry 4,1,3,3,)

13. Ibid. p.99 (2,5,4,1/ 2,5,3,3)

14. Hans Richter Dada: Art and Anti-Art

15. Scientists Who Believe Moody Press,1984 Edited Eric Barrett& David Fisher p164

16. Clifford Plopper Chinese Religion Seen Through the Proverb New York Paragon Book Reprint, 1969 p.74

17. Psalm 130:3-4

18. Lao Tse Tao Te Ching Penguin Classics,p.114

19. Analects Middlesex, England: Penguin Classics Translated D.C.Lau 1963 p.73

Chapter Three

1. Wu En Bo Wo Weisheme Xin Shang Di p.11

2. Analects Middlesex, England: Penguin Classics Translated D.C.Lau 1963 p.81

3. Ibid. p.73

4. Ibid. p.61

5. Ibid. p.80

6. Ibid. p.88

7. Ibid. p.105

8. Ibid. p.87

9. Ibid. p.140 16-8

10. Ibid.p.69

11. Ibid. p.69 3-11

12. Chen JingPan Confucius as a Teacher Beijing Foreign Language Press, p.170

13. Ibid.177

14. William Edgar Geil The Great Wall of China Stureon&Walton Co.:1909

15. Sima Qian Records of the Grand Historian of China translated Burton Watson

16. Ibid.

17. Chen JingPan Confucius as a Teacher Beijing Foreign Language Press,quoting Book of Poetry 22,5,8,4

18. Ibid. quoting Yung-Chi Hoe p.278

Chapter Four

1. Jung Chang Wild Swans: Three Daughters of China New York: Anchor Books, 1992 p.30
2. Ibid p.34
3. Jackie Pullinger Chasing the Dragon
4. Chen JingPan Confucius as a Teacher Beijing Foreign Language Press,p.279-280
5. Taikaaki Aikawa Unwilling Patriot
6. William Edgar Geil The Great Wall of China Stureon&Walton Co.:1909 p.30
7. Gao Yuan Born Red A Chronicle of the Cultural Revolution Stanford University Press 1987 p.119
8. Ibid. p.123
9. Quoting Mao on Contradictions p.46-47, 62
10. Sources of Chinese Tradition William M. Bary, Ed. New York: Columbia University Press 1960 p.118

Chapter Five

1. John 19:26-7
2. Exodus 20:12
3. NIV Study Bible
4. Proverbs 23'22,25
5. Leviticus 19:32
6. Exodus 20:4
7. Isaiah 49:6
8. Isaiah 9:7
9. Isaiah 9:6
10. Isaiah 61:1
11. Isaiah 9:7
12. Micah 5:2
13. Mark 2:11
14. Mark 7:34
15. Matthew 10:4-6
16. Luke 20:25
17. John 18:36
18. Lao Tse Tao Te Ching Penguin Classics p.63
19. Mark 10:42-45
20. John 6:35
21. John 8:12
22. Matthew 9:12
23. John 5:21
24. John 5:39
25. Mark 2:28

26. Mark 2:5
27. Matthew 12:6
28. Matthew 7:28-29
29. John 19:10
30. Mark 14:61
31. Christianity Today Robert Coles
32. Scott Peck Further Along the Road Less Traveled New York: Simon & Schuster 1993 p.189
33. John 5:19
34. Luke 22:42
35. Mark 15:34

Chapter Six

1. Taisuke Mitamura Chinese Eunuchs: The Structure of Intimate Politics Tokyo: Charles E.Tuttle Co., 1992 p.120-122
2. Fortune Magazine October 31, 1994 (The New Power in Asia)
3. Confucius as a Teacher, p.299, quoting Mencius, 1,17,12
4. Chinese Eunuchs p.74
5. Bill Holm Coming Home Crazy Milkweed Editions, 1990

Chapter Seven

1. Tucker N. Callaway From Zen Way, Jesus Way Tokyo: Charles E. Tuttle Co. 1976 p.65 quoting Hann-ya-shin-gyo
2. Feng Yu-Lan A Short History of Chinese Philosophy New York: The Free Press, 1948 p.271
3. Sacred Books of the Buddhists Milanda's Questions Luzac&Co, 1964 p.96
4. Ching Hai The Key to Immediate Enlightenment Wu Shang Shi p14-15)

Chapter Eight

1. John Blofeld The Boddhisattva of Compassion-the Mystical tradition of Kuan Yin Shambhala Press p.114)
2. E. T. C. Werner Myths and Legends of China p.252
3. John Blofeld The Boddhisattva of Compassion-the Mystical tradition of Kuan Yin Shambhala Press p.114)
4. C. N. Tay Kuan Yin: the Cult of Half Asia Taipei: She Tuan Fa Ben Hui p.37-38
5. See Burton Day Popular Religion in Pre-Communist China p.51
6. Feng Yu-Lan A Short History of Chinese Philosophy New York: The Free Press, 1948 p.62 from Chuang Tsu

7. C. N. Tay Kuan Yin: the Cult of Half Asia Taipei: She Tuan Fa Ben Hui p.113
8. Ibid.
9. John Blofeld The Boddhisattva of Compassion-the Mystical tradition of Kuan Yin Shambhala Press (from Forward)
10. Aeropagus Magazine Yves Raguin
11. Feng Yu-Lan A Short History of Chinese Philosophy New York: The Free Press, 1948
12. Ibid. p.3
13. Ibid. p. 327

Chapter Nine

1. Robert W. Faid A Scientific Approach to Biblical Mysteries New Leaf Press, 1993
2. Matthew 2:1-2
3. Genesis 1:27-31
4. Thomas Howard Christ, the Tiger Wheaton, Illinois: Harold Shaw Publishers, 1967 p.92
5. Genesis 2:18
6. Genesis 12:2-3
7. Isaiah 19:2
8. Isaiah 49:6
9. Isaiah 9:6
10. Isaiah 53:3-5
11. One Destiny from The Most Famous Jew Of All Lederer Publications 1989
12. Luke 22:44
13. China Spring

Chapter Ten

1. Humanist Magazine: Kerry Temple, "Who Do You Say That I Am?" May/June 1991 quoting Thomas Sheehan p.12
2. Humanist Magazine: Kerry Temple, "Who Do You Say That I Am?" May/June 1991 quoting John Collins p.12
3. Gary Eisenberg Smashing the Idols: A Jewish Inquiry Into the Cult Phenomena Northvale, New Jersey: Jason Aronson Inc., 1988 p.169
4. Life Magazine December 1994 p.68
5. A.N.Wilson Jesus, a Life New York: W.W.Norton & Co. Inc.,1992 p.47
6. Rudolf Bultmann The History of the Synoptic Tradition p.372-373
7. Of Fernseed and Elephants C.S.Lewis from Evidence That Demands a Verdict II Apendix

8. Matthew 8:27
9. Japan Times December 29, 1994
10. H.G.Creel Confucius and the Chinese Way p.292 Harper&Row 1949
11. Matthew 11:3
12: Matthew 12:24
13. Humanist Magazine: Kerry Temple, "Who Do You Say That I Am?"
    May/June 1991
14. Gary Eisenberg Smashing the Idols: A Jewish Inquiry Into the Cult
    Phenomena Northvale, New Jersey: Jason Aronson Inc., 1988 p.169
15. Humanist Magazine: Kerry Temple, "Who Do You Say That I Am?"
    May/June 1991
16. Japan Times December 29, 1994
17. Chen JingPan Confucius as a Teacher Beijing Foreign Language Press
    p.110
18. H.G.Creel Confucius and the Chinese Way p.292 Harper&Row 1949
19. U.S.News&World Report October 1994
20. A.N.Wilson Jesus, a Life New York: W.W.Norton & Co. Inc.,1992
    p.66
21. John 20:27

Chapter Eleven

1. Bill Holm Coming Home Crazy Bill Holms Milkweed Editions, 1990
2. Jung Chang Wild Swans: Three Daughters of China New York:
    Anchor Books, 1992 p.21
3. Bill Holm Coming Home Crazy Bill Holms Milkweed Editions, 1990
    p.53

Chapter Twelve

1. Genesis 2:17
2. Chinese Eunuchs: The Structure of Internal Politics Tokyo: Charles
    Tuttle Co., 1963 p.48
3. Chinese Eunuchs: The Structure of Internal Politics Tokyo: Charles
    Tuttle Co., 1963
4. Analects Middlesex, England: Penguin Classics Translated D.C.Lau
    1963
5. Sources of Chinese Tradition Vol.1 New York: Columbia University
    Press, 1960 (William Theodore De Bary Editor) MoZi
6. Ibid.
7. Isaiah 53:6
8. Analects Middlesex, England: Penguin Classics Translated D.C.Lau
    1963 p.69 3-13

9. Chen JingPan Confucius as a Teacher Beijing Foreign Language Press p.99 from Book of History 2,4
10. Ibid. p.101
11. Ibid. p.104 from Tso Chuan
12. John 10:7-10

Chapter Thirteen

1. Luke 10:24
2. Luke 12:4-5
3. Exodus 3:6
4. Isaiah 6:5
5. Job 42:5-6
6. Daniel 10:7-17
7. Charisma Magazine
8. C.L.Culpepper The Shantung Revival Crescendo Book Publishing p.44. Also a book of the same name by Mary Crawford, p.47.
9. Charisma Magazine
10. Isaiah 53:5
11. Luke 23:33
12. Romans 3:23
13. Luke 23:39
14. Luke 23:40-43
15. Matthew 27:50-51

Chapter Fourteen:

1. Sima Qian Records of the Grand Historian of China translated Burton Watson p.46
2. William Edgar Geil The Great Wall of China Stureon&Walton Co.:1909
3. Sima Qian Records of the Grand Historian of China translated Burton Watson p.62/63
4. Emily M. Ahern The Cult of the Dead in a Chinese Village Stanford University Press p.117
5. Deuteronomy 18:10-11
6. Luke 23:28
7. A.N.Wilson Jesus, a Life New York: W.W.Norton & Co. Inc.,1992
8. Humanist Magazine: Kerry Temple, "Who Do You Say That I Am?" May/June 1991
9. Luke 24:36-39
10. John 20:27
11. I. Corinthians 15:3-8
12. Josh Mcdowell More Than a Carperter p.96

To order additional copies of **True Son of Heaven**
please send $9.00* + $2.00 for shipping and handling to:

Kuai Mu Press
6765 37th SW
Seattle, WA 98126

For quantity discounts please call
(206) 935-6265

*Washington residents add 8.2% sales tax

For Canadian orders, please send $12.00 + 7% GST + $3.00
for shipping and handling.